EDUCATION for EMPLOYABILITY

Rewarding Learning

FOR CCEA GCSE LEARNING FOR LIFE AND WORK

Verona Hassan
Dorothy Wilson

HODDER
EDUCATION
PART OF HACHETTE LIVRE UK

The publishers would like to thank the following individuals, institutions and companies for permission to reproduce copyright illustrations in this book: p7 Macduff Everton/Corbis; p8 Tesco; p9 Ditty's Home Bakery; p10l Archivo Iconografico, S.A./Corbis, r Anthony Cooper, Ecoscene/Corbis; p12, p20, p22, p54 Peter Keogh; p13t Alison Wright/Corbis, b BDI Images Ltd; p15tl, bl Michael St. Maur Sheil/Corbis, tr, br Joan Shannon; p17l Investors in People, r www.ni-charter.gov.uk; p18 Geray Sweeney/Corbis; p24 Rex Features; p28 North East Institute of Further & Higher Education; p34 Sipa Press/ Rex Features; p36 tl Bettman/Corbis, tr Michael Barley/Corbis, b Jagadeesh Nv/Reuters/Corbis; p42 Reuters/Corbis; p44r Invest Northern Ireland, l Fermanagh Enterprise; p45 and p50 Shell LiveWIRE; p46 Kilcronaghan Activity and Conference Centre; p47 Johnny Buzzerio/Corbis; p49 Alan Stone © BBC Worldwide; p57 Tayto, Ulster Bank, Marks & Spencer; p58 Charlie Munsey/Corbis; p59 Cardinale Stephane/Corbis Sygma.

The publishers would also like to thank the following for copyright material in this book: p11 News Letter, Northern Ireland; p14 United Dairies; p16 and p47 Belfast Telegraph; p23 www.bbc.co.uk; p25 Department of Finance and Personnel; p50 Aisling Collins/Shell LiveWIRE.

Every effort has been made to trace and acknowledge ownership of copyright. The publishers will be glad to make suitable arrangements with any copyright holders whom it has not been possible to contact.

Note about the Internet links in the book. The user should be aware that URLs or web addresses change regularly. Every effort has been made to ensure the accuracy of the URLs provided in this book on going to press. It is inevitable, however, that some will change. It is sometimes possible to find a relocated web page, by just typing in the address of the home page for a website in the URL window of your browser.

Hodder Headline's policy is to use papers that are natural, renewable and recyclable products and made from wood grown in sustainable forests. The logging and manufacturing processes are expected to conform to the environmental regulations of the country of origin.

Orders: please contact Bookpoint Ltd, 130 Milton Park, Abingdon, Oxon OX14 4SB. Telephone: (44) 01235 827720. Fax: (44) 01235 400454. Lines are open from 9.00 – 5.00, Monday to Saturday, with a 24-hour message answering service. You can also order through our website www.hoddereducation.co.uk.

British Library Cataloguing in Publication Data
A catalogue record for this title is available from the British Library

ISBN-13: 978 0 340 86917 8

First Published 2004
Impression number 10 9 8 7 6
Year 2010, 2009, 2008

Cover photo from getty images/photographer Antonio Mo.
Layout design by Jenny Fleet. Artwork by Steve Parkhouse at Daedalus Studios.
Printed in Italy for Hodder Education an imprint of Hachette Livre Uk,
338 Euston Road, London NW1 3BH.

Contents

Introduction

Employability is a relatively new term and, while no common widely accepted definition yet exists, there is agreement that developing employability is one essential element in building a competitive economy. The Confederation of British Industry has proposed the following definition of employability:

> **The possession by an individual of the qualities and competencies required to meet the changing needs of employers and customers and thereby help to realise his/her aspirations and potential in work.**

This means that you need to be able to develop the skills required to get and keep a job and to have the ability to build a career and succeed in the ever-changing workplace.

Qualities and competences which make up employability

- values and attitudes compatible with the work – including a desire to learn, to apply that learning, to improve and to take advantage of change
- basic skills (literacy and numeracy)
- key skills (communication, application of numbers, information technology, improving one's own learning and performance, working with others, problem solving) sufficient for the needs of the work
- other generic skills that are becoming increasingly 'key' (e.g., modern language and customer service skills)
- up-to-date and relevant knowledge and understanding of the work
- up-to-date job-specific skills
- the ability to manage one's own career

Source: Based on 'In search of Employability', CBI 1998

It is important to develop these qualities and competences because today's labour market is flexible and changeable.

Centuries ago, choosing a career was a simple process. Skills were handed down from one generation to the next. People were self-sufficient, working on farms and producing their own food and clothing. Jobs were done when the need arose, and payment was often in the form of exchange of services.

By the end of the nineteenth century, people began working for wages. A person's job was usually his/her 'career' for life.

Now, in the twenty-first century, traditional industries, such as craft and manufacturing, are being replaced by a knowledge-based economy. This is part of an international movement that is transforming work patterns and the nature of skills required by employees.

To be competent in a knowledge-based economy you need to know how to access information from a variety of sources and make sense of that information.

The aim of *Education for Employability* is to ensure that all young people develop personal qualities, skills, knowledge, understanding and attitudes which will give them a strong foundation for lifelong learning and work in a rapidly changing economic environment. The book is divided into three sections:

- Work in the Local and Global Economy (pages 6–25)
- Personal Career Planning (pages 26–41)
- Enterprise and Entrepreneurship (pages 42–62).

Introduction

In order to survive in today's economic climate, many businesses in Northern Ireland have had to broaden their market area. This has meant that companies are now entering new markets at a global level. This section examines changes in the local and global economy and employment trends. It explores how consumer choices and environmental considerations affect work issues in the local and global economy, and the financial constraints within which individuals, organisations, businesses and the government make choices. More importantly, this section is intended to make you more aware of how these issues affect your personal career decisions. During your work you should continually ask yourself: 'What does this mean for my career?'

1. Changes in the local and global economy

Types of economy

Each country has an economic system that is concerned with:

- how production should be organised (e.g., how many workers should be employed, and how goods and services should be allocated to individuals)
- what and how much should be produced (e.g., how much food should be produced).

Countries choose to organise their economies differently, so there are a number of different types of economic systems. Some examples are given in the table below.

Nowadays, businesses operate within their:

- local economy
- national economy

- **global economy** (i.e., the economies of other countries throughout the world).

The local economy

Tesco are a large supermarket chain that operate at a local level. They provide a service for the local community by selling a range of products. They create a variety of job opportunities in the local community, and occasionally buy some products that have been locally produced (e.g., strawberries, mushrooms and potatoes).

The national economy

Tesco also operate at a national level, as they have hundreds of stores throughout the United Kingdom.

They have to react to national changes in demand for their products (e.g., an increased demand for **organic** products). They also have to take account of regional factors. For example, consumers' incomes could

Type of economy	Definition	Country
Free market economy	Economy where goods and services are produced in line with demand from consumers.	USA and Japan
Planned economy	Economy where resources are allocated by the government through a system of planning, where goods and services are produced to satisfy the needs of all citizens of the country, not just those who have the money to pay.	China
Mixed economy	Economy where some goods and services are produced in line with the demand from consumers, but others are provided by the government (e.g., health services).	Ireland, France and Great Britain

Which of these products do you think are locally produced?

change if a number of factories close down in a particular area, as this causes unemployment, resulting in people having less money to spend. The lack of money available then affects the profits of businesses in that area. As a national business, Tesco would probably be able to take a profit reduction in an individual area without suffering too much; however, a small business in the area would be likely to struggle because of such a change in the local economy.

National businesses like Tesco have to consider the competition from other large supermarket outlets throughout the country, as well as competition from smaller, local businesses. As a large national business they are able to buy products in bulk from suppliers and offer goods to the consumer at competitive prices.

The global economy

Most businesses are likely to be affected by the global economy. A lot of businesses export their goods and services to other countries, and many businesses import products from other countries.

There are many reasons why businesses import products from other countries, including:

climate some countries (e.g., Spain and those in South America) can produce oranges or bananas that cannot be produced in Northern Ireland, which is why they are imported for sale here.

cost in some countries (e.g., China, Korea and Poland), workers are prepared to work for very low wages. This means that it is cheaper for some businesses to have their goods produced in these countries, even with the added transport costs.

Of course, as these goods are being transported around the world – by air, sea and land – there is an environmental issue to be aware of: polluting the atmosphere. (See also page 15.)

Tesco offer their customers a wide range of products throughout their stores nationwide. They are able to do this because they import these products from different countries around the world; they are therefore part of the global economy.

Consumer items can come from all over the world.

Getting your custom

Business organisations from a local level through to a global level are in competition for customers. When you go to buy a new pair of trainers, you buy from the many brands that are on offer to you. It is a very competitive market and businesses have to promote their products in order to gain your custom.

They do this in numerous ways. They run advertising campaigns through the media (e.g., on television, radio, or in national and local newspapers, through poster campaigns and through advertising leaflets direct to householders). They have sales promotions on certain items. They offer discount vouchers or loyalty vouchers where points are given with each purchase (which add up to an amount of money over a period of time). Large businesses often run competitions where customers could win a holiday or free flight.

The customer can benefit from this competition between businesses by getting a choice of products at a discount price, a free gift, or an opportunity to win a prize. However, it costs money for a company to mount an advertising campaign, and it may, in the long term, increase the cost of the product for the customer.

Large organisations have the money to promote the products on a bigger scale. This could have the effect of decreasing sales for the small businesses that cannot afford to mount campaigns in this way.

Tesco are one of many supermarkets that reward customers with points for every purchase they make.

activity

You have seen an advertisement, placed by your local supermarket, offering part-time jobs packing shelves. You would like to apply for one of these jobs and want to do some background research about the supermarket beforehand.

Write a short report under the following headings:

◆ Name of the supermarket (choose a supermarket that you know and that your family uses)

◆ The local economy (explain how your chosen supermarket supports the local economy – for example, find out how many people it employs)

◆ The global economy (visit the supermarket, or examine labels on food at home, and explain how this supermarket operates in the global economy).

Think global ... act local

In 1963, the doors of Ditty's Home Bakery opened for the first time in a small rural village, 40 miles from Belfast. This is a family business: Mr and Mrs Ditty were joined by their son, Robert, in 1977, who took over the running of the bakery, along with his wife and sister, soon after. In 1996 his nephew also joined the family business. In Robert Ditty's own words:

> 'Our success is based on the principles of craft baking, innovation, strict quality control and great service. We aim to give our customers quality bakery products at reasonable prices.'

Ditty's Home Bakery, Magherafelt.

Innovation

Ditty's Home Bakery have grown by constant **innovation** and development of products, which brings about a wide and sophisticated choice of bakery products and the very latest in continental thinking. They supply local supermarkets and you can sample their products in their own café in Magherafelt.

International success – a product that does travel

Ditty's Home Bakery concentrate on speciality **niche markets**; they therefore have a high level of expertise, which is in great demand. Their markets include kosher food and exports to the USA, Italy and Japan.

They believe in getting back to basics, using the best ingredients, and following the recipes and methods of their grandmother's generation, but on a larger scale. They recently imported sultanas from grapes grown in Australia, and flour from a small family-owned mill in Scotland.

Changing employment trends

Businesses must decide how and where they produce goods and services. This is influenced by:

◆ advances in technology
◆ availability of workers with the right skills
◆ the wages that workers are willing to accept.

All of these need to be considered when mapping your career path and understanding the knowledge and skills that you will need to develop in order to be employable in the twenty-first century.

activities

Read the case study above about Ditty's Home Bakery, which is located in a small rural community and operates in both the local and global economy. Then answer the following questions:

1. How does this company support the local economy?

2. Why is it successful?

3. How are Ditty's Home Bakery involved in the global economy?

4. What is meant by 'speciality niche markets'?

5. What do you think are the workers' main skills and qualities that enable this business to operate in both the local and global economy?

An image of farming from medieval times (above). How do farming methods differ today (right)?

Technology

Technology is constantly changing and these changes bring about a change in the jobs and skills that are required in a workforce. **Automated assembly lines** are now commonplace in factories that are mass-producing products (e.g., video recorders, DVD players, computer components, cars, etc.). In an assembly line, goods are made in stages from start to finish by computer-operated machinery. Goods that are made in large quantities (**mass production**) are usually made by this method with groups of workers concentrating on one area of production. In modern factories, the use of technology and robots means that the job of the production worker is often not manual labour, but is focused on operating computerised machinery and recording information.

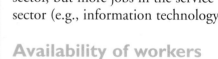

Computer-aided design has helped companies to have products designed in one country, produced in another and sold in the global marketplace.

The above label comes from a pair of trousers bought in Northern Ireland. You can see that the trousers were designed in Germany but made in Poland.

Information and communication technology has transformed the service industries. It has allowed companies to keep vast amounts of information stored on computers and enabled workers to communicate throughout the world, by using e-mail, video-conferencing and the Internet.

While technology can increase the amount of goods produced, ensure quality control, make factory environments cleaner and safer places to work, and speed up communications, it has changed the types of work available and the skills required.

Because of the developments in technology there are now fewer jobs in the manufacturing sector, but more jobs in the service sector (e.g., information technology).

Availability of workers

Because companies in Northern Ireland are continuing to get goods produced in other countries, where labour is cheaper, many employees of traditional manufacturing industries are having to learn new skills for the service sector. For this reason, it is important for you, as you map out your career path, to take account of the trends that exist within your local labour market, so that you arrange to learn the correct skills.

Workers' wages

Companies based in Northern Ireland decide to have their goods produced in other countries because workers in Asia and Eastern European countries, such as Poland, work for much less than is acceptable in Northern Ireland. The cost of production is therefore cheaper. However, the quality of the finished goods might not always meet the standard of those produced locally.

If a member of your family is employed in a factory that decides to have some of its products manufactured abroad, he/she could face losing their job, with the prospect of having to retrain to be employable in today's technological market place.

Movement of workers

Not only are companies now moving much of their manufacturing to other countries where labour costs are cheaper, but Northern Ireland businesses are employing workers from other countries to do the job in the local community. This is because they either have skills that are missing in the local community or because they are willing to do work that others are not. Among these workers are nurses from the Philippines and factory workers from Portugal, who make up 10 per cent of the Dungannon working population.

activities

Read the following newspaper extract:

POSSIBLE JOB LOSSES ADDS TO TEXTILE INDUSTRY WOES

... Meanwhile, it has emerged that some workers at the Saville Row shirt company in Castledawson will be issued with redundancy notices next week. The 40-year-old company which manufactures shirts for the upmarket retailer Thomas Pink, confirmed on Tuesday that it is axing 65 of its 185 strong workforce as it transfers production abroad. Managing director Edmund Douglas said the remaining jobs should be secure, but added it would depend on consumer demand for locally manufactured products. Commenting on the recent crisis in the sector, which has seen the number of redundancies soar to 450 over the last fortnight, Mid-Ulster MLA Billy Armstrong says the Government must intervene to protect Northern Ireland's remaining textile jobs.

'The textile industry used to be the foundation of Ulster's manufacturing base. Now it has become an ever-shrinking sector, which in many people's view is not a stable employment area ...'

Source: from *News Letter* 6 February, 2003

Now answer these questions on the extract:

1. Why do you think this company has decided to take their manufacturing to another country?

2. What effect do you think this will have on the local community?

3. What new skills do you think the workers who are going to be made redundant need to develop in order to get another job?

2. Consumer choices and the environment

This unit outlines how consumer choices and environmental considerations affect work issues in the local and global economy.

Consumer choices

As consumers, we demand choice. In any large supermarket in Northern Ireland, alongside locally produced Armagh apples, there will be two or three varieties of English apple, different varieties from France, New Zealand, South Africa and North America, and at least two varieties of 'organic' apple. This whole range is carried by the supermarket because of consumer demand. Consumers who are denied choice will shop elsewhere.

Why do we choose one variety of apple over all the others? Our choice may be determined by:

◆ the amount of money we have available to spend

◆ taste preference

◆ appearance preference

◆ brand loyalty

◆ a wish to support local suppliers

◆ a determination not to support those exploiting workers

◆ a wish to buy chemical-free produce.

We make a choice each time we buy goods or services. This choice may be influenced by:

◆ what we hear and see on the radio and television, either as part of a programme or as an advertisement

◆ what we read in newspapers and magazines

◆ advertisements around us

◆ what friends recommend

◆ our own experiences.

activity

As a group, imagine you are going to buy new jeans and a personal CD player. List what will influence your choice.

Support for local industry

Consumers demand choice.

We may strongly support the idea of 'buy Northern Ireland', believing that we ought to buy goods produced locally to support our local economy. What happens, however, when goods cannot be produced here as cheaply as in a developing country? Are we prepared to pay over twice as much for a shirt made in Ballymena as for one made in Bangladesh? The vast majority of us would not be prepared to do this. We consider value for money to be one of the main priorities when choosing what we buy.

We had a well-established textile industry in Northern Ireland. These textile factories produced clothes and household goods for local, national and international markets with success. Unfortunately, the use of a much cheaper workforce by competitors in a developing country made it impossible for home manufacturers to compete in the marketplace. Consumers may have been concerned about the increase in unemployment as textile workers were made redundant, or about the effect of the job losses on the local economy, but they were not prepared to pay extra in order to buy locally produced goods.

Goods are cheaper to buy when production costs are very low.

activities

1. Make a list of the country of manufacture for five items of your clothing.
2. As a group, compile a list of the countries of origin and identify the location of these countries on an atlas. From the information about the countries in the atlas, or perhaps from further information you could get from the Internet, suggest reasons why the goods were manufactured there.

Consumers dictate

There are many other examples of how the power of consumers to make choices influences both the local and global economy.

For example, after the bombing of the World Trade Center on September 11, 2001, airlines found it almost impossible to sell tickets on some routes. Even with incredible reductions consumers were not prepared to buy tickets to fly to some destinations. Initially, this resulted in reduced schedules, but aircrafts were later withdrawn from service and many airline employees across the world lost their jobs. Even though thousands of people were being made redundant, consumers could not be persuaded to fly to long-haul destinations as they had done previously.

Another example is how we are much more aware these days of the food we consume. By law, food products must have labels detailing their contents, country of origin, use-by date and any warnings, such as 'may contain traces of nut'. This allows us to choose food with care and sometimes even to influence the production of food through what we buy. For example:

◆ consumer demand has brought about an increase in the range and choice of organic foodstuff in larger supermarkets

◆ organised objection to the introduction of **genetically modified crops** has pushed the government to review the effect of GM crops before allowing their production in the United Kingdom.

Changes in fashion also create different demands from consumers. The change in trend from carpet to wooden flooring brought about the demise of some carpet manufacturers who did not foresee this change in consumer demand and adjust their manufacturing process to meet it (e.g., by increasing the production of rugs and reducing the production of carpets). Greater awareness of the effect of our diet has changed what food we eat. Manufacturers have responded with producing 'healthy' alternatives which meet the requirements of today's health-conscious consumer.

Healthy alternatives demanded by consumers.

United poised to lead dairy innovation

PRESS RELEASE

A £4.5 million investment by leading dairy business, **United Dairy Farmers** – parent company of Dale Farm – is to signal an exciting new era in dairy food innovation and secure the company's position at the forefront of the dairy-food market.

Opened on 13 October by Ian Pearson MP, NIO Minister for the Economy and Agriculture ... the Group Technical Centre at Pennybridge in Ballymena ... will house the United Group's research and development team and facilities.

Speaking at the launch, Group Chief Executive David Dobbin explained that the £4.5 million investment is fundamental to United's strategy to develop a world-class dairy business, capable of meeting the intense competitive challenges of the global dairy-food marketplace and enhancing the financial return for the Group and its farmer members.

'Our strategy [is to] focus instead on

- the value-added food ingredients such as grated cheese for both food manufacturers and the catering industry,
- food service such as individual portions of butter, milk or cream for the catering industry and
- **retail** markets of milk, cheese, yoghurts, ice cream, etc. for shops and supermarkets to sell as individual items to consumers

is paying off, leading to considerable growth during 2002/03.

'However, added value markets themselves are increasingly over-crowded and our future success will depend on our ability to provide innovative dairy products which consumers want and need. This will be significantly enhanced by the capability provided by this new Centre and the talented team of people who will work in it.

'These resources put United's food processing subsidiary, Dale Farm, in pole position to become a recognised leader in the areas of product innovation, quality and consumer choice, within the domestic, EU and wider global dairy food market.

'Investment at this level is essential if we are to compete with the world's best, and it will enhance our ability to respond rapidly to customers who are increasingly demanding new and different taste experiences from products that are also competitively priced.'

The investment at Pennybridge is part of an ongoing £20 million plus investment programme by United, which recently saw the commissioning of a new £3 million milk evaporation facility and £2 million cheese packing and whey processing unit at the Group's Dunmanbridge milk processing plant near Cookstown.

Source: press release on United Dairies website, www.utdni.co.uk, 13 October 2003 (adapted)

activities

Read the above press release and answer the following questions:

1. What type of new facility was United Dairy Farmers opening?

2. What kind of employment opportunities do you think would be provided at this facility?

3. What type of employment opportunities do you think would be provided by the Cookstown facility?

4. What factors would have been taken into account in deciding the locations of both of these facilities?

5. What must United Dairy Farmers do in order to maintain or expand its share of the dairy business?

Caring for the environment

As individuals, we are concerned with environmental issues. We do not like to witness the destruction of our environment. We like to feel that manufacturers, in their extraction of **raw materials**, in their disposal of waste materials and in the goods they produce for us to buy, cause no harm to the environment. Groups such as Greenpeace try to raise public awareness of the dangers of pollution.

We must protect our environment today for others to enjoy tomorrow.

A rise in public concern often pressurises government into **action** resulting in the passing of anti-pollution legislation. The implementation of this legislation

may result in increased production costs that, ultimately, will have to be borne by consumers.

For example, the United Kingdom government has promised to meet certain reductions in carbon dioxide emissions and, as a result, is imposing nationwide controls on emissions from power stations. There are three power stations in Northern Ireland; two of these already have modern gas-fired plants that meet government requirements. It is, however, a different matter at Kilroot, the third power station, which burns coal and oil and provides Northern Ireland with 25 per cent of its electricity. The costs involved in modernising Kilroot in order to meet the government requirements will have to be borne by the consumers and will result in prices for electricity being forced to increase.

Emissions from Kilroot power station must be reduced!

The environment and work

At times, protecting our environment may affect work issues. Examples include:

◆ When stocks of a particular type of fish are at risk from over-fishing, quotas on fishing fleets are enforced by agriculture ministers. This may result in a limit on the number of days that fishing fleets are permitted to fish.

◆ The proposed mining for lignite in north Antrim would provide employment in the area but is, nevertheless, being strongly opposed by locals due to the destruction of the environment.

◆ The proposed wind farm off the north coast at Portstewart strand would be environmentally friendly and provide pollution-free power but it would also infringe on the beauty of the area which may reduce the number of tourists and result in a decrease in employment in the local tourist industry.

Portstewart strand. Is this the right location for an off-shore wind farm?

Consumers create change

Nowadays, we are much more aware of the effect of our actions on the environment. Environmental matters are constantly being brought to our attention. For example, we are encouraged to reduce, reuse and recycle waste materials, to be aware of gas emissions and to dispose of litter properly. This knowledge and awareness is influential when we buy goods, making us want only goods that are environmentally friendly. Consumers in general like to consider that they are environmentally and **socially responsible**.

Consumers have the power to effect change by exercising their right to choice. Business exists to meet consumer demand. To be successful it has to stock the goods or provide the service demanded by consumers. When consumers change trends by exercising their power, the industry has to react to this change. This may involve:

◆ a change in production methods to meet the new demands

◆ reduction in the output to allow for change in demand

◆ closure of a production plant because there is no longer a demand for the product.

The outcome of any of these alternatives is change for those who are employed. Employees may have to retrain to take part in the production of new lines, or they may be made redundant and have to seek new employment. Seeking new employment may also require retraining. We live in an increasingly technological age which requires a well-trained, adaptable workforce. Workers have to seek new skills, change work patterns, and be more mobile, flexible and adaptable.

Consumers' demands also change as they progress through life, or as society changes. Producers must keep up-to-date with these demands. For example, we have an ageing population, which means that more people are living longer. This, combined with better health care, pension schemes and a greater awareness of the need for a healthy lifestyle, has produced a new consumer group of active people with time available for interests and hobbies. Producers must ensure that the goods and services required by this niche group are available to meet consumer demand.

Time consultants on the way in jobs shake-up

NEW JOBS – such as time consultants, who help people organise their busy lives – are set to be created under a transformation of the employment market, according to a new report.

Scientific work is also expected to grow, as will jobs for pilots, because of a predicted growth in air travel.

Work for so-called 'longevity consultants' could emerge, to help retired people keep healthy and fit in their later years.

Vocational awards body City & Guilds said other jobs set to increase would include personal dieticians, psychologists and plastic surgeons.

Source: *Belfast Telegraph*, 30 October 2003

activity

Read the above newspaper extract. As a group, discuss why you think the introduction of the new jobs mentioned and the predicted growth in the other jobs is likely to happen. Remember to consider the effects of consumer choice.

How may I help you?

In today's increasingly competitive marketplace consumers demand service as well as choice. If businesses are to succeed they must provide a first-class service to their consumers. Businesses try to do this through:

◆ the manner in which employees greet and attend to customers

◆ the helpfulness of employees to customers

◆ the appearance of employees (often by wearing a uniform)

◆ the employees' knowledge of the products being sold

◆ the after-sales service being provided

◆ the appearance of the premises

◆ the cleanliness of the premises.

Employees who come into contact with customers play a prime role in the provision of service. In order to do this well they have to be properly trained in all aspects of customer service.

Investors in People

Many businesses seek nationally recognised endorsement from 'Investors in People', the independent government-funded body responsible for evaluating the quality of training and personal development offered to employees (www.iipuk.co.uk). These standards provide employees with the opportunity to become fully integrated, committed, developed and effective within the organisation.

Business organisations as a whole become more effective when the workforce is totally committed. They often encourage employees to achieve standards and targets by operating award schemes such as 'employee of the month'. At other times greater success can be achieved through the development of good teamwork and often targets are set for a team of employees, rather than for an individual, to achieve.

INVESTORS IN PEOPLE

Charter Mark

CUSTOMER SERVICE EXCELLENCE

Within public services – organisations such as libraries, hospitals, clinics, GP surgeries, schools, government offices and local council services – excellence of service can be recognised by a Charter Mark. Charter Mark is an award given by a government agency to a public service organisation in recognition of its standard of service. To achieve a Charter Mark, an organisation must show that it has set high performance standards in the service it gives, is continually trying to improve its service and that its staff are courteous, helpful and responsive to its consumers.

A Charter Mark is awarded for a three-year period. After this the organisation must reapply to be **accredited**. By setting this time limit, Charter Mark awards ensure that public service organisations continually strive for improvement.

activities

1. Take a look around your local community. How many businesses or public service organisations can you find that have the endorsement of Investor in People or Charter Mark? You might find this information in reception areas or on company headed paper.

2. Does your school have either of these awards? Can you find out what had to be done in order to achieve this award?

The Investors in People and Charter Mark agencies are only examples of how businesses strive to achieve accredited standards within their organisation in order to compete. As future employers or employees it is important for each of us to recognise the necessity of high quality in terms of performance at work.

Quality performance in terms of work is something we can start now. Completing work accurately and promptly to the best of our ability, taking pride in the work we produce, looking after books and equipment and working as a team member are all qualities that, once developed, will transfer readily to the workplace.

17

This unit outlines the financial constraints under which the individual, organisations, businesses and the government must make choices.

The individual's choices

Spending money

Today, we have much more money to spend than was available when our grandparents were teenagers but we also have many more demands on our money. Years ago, goods such as PlayStations, GameBoys or mobile phones were not available; there was not such a choice in clothes and shoes, nor were there five-screen cinemas, multi-activity sports centres or ice hockey venues. Teenagers had less money but they had less choice of goods available to spend it on.

Today, although we have wide choices available to us, the same situation exists as in our grandparents' day: we are held back by the amount of money we have available to spend.

As children, we rely on our parents for pocket money. As teenagers and students, this can be supplemented if we get a part-time job after school, or at weekends, and full time during holidays. Later, we can enter full-time employment, when the amount of money we receive is called our income.

Odyssey Arena Belfast. This is just one of many places to spend your money.

Commitments

As we progress through life our income becomes larger – but so also do our commitments. A child receiving only pocket money has no commitment to that money other than self-enjoyment. On the other hand, students who possibly have income from parents as well as what they are able to earn may have to pay for living accommodation, food, heating and clothes before they can think of self-enjoyment.

Later in life, commitments become even greater as we perhaps buy a car, marry, set up home and have a family. This brings commitments too: paying for a mortgage, **income tax**, rates, insurances, heating, food, holidays, clothes, electricity, car repayments – and the list goes on. Some of these items are necessary to live (e.g., food) while others are luxuries we want (e.g., holidays) in order to make life more pleasant.

We all have items that we must pay for weekly or monthly. These are our commitments. The amount we have left over is our disposable income: what we are free to spend on what we like.

activities

James has recently started work as a junior reporter on a local paper. His annual salary is £15,000. James estimates that 30 per cent of his salary will be used to meet his income tax, national insurance and pension each month. He shares an apartment with three friends and his monthly contribution to living expenses is £250. In addition to this he pays £130 each month for a car loan and £29 each month for gym membership.

1. How much disposable income does James have each month?

2. James has seen an advertisement for a holiday to Florida direct from Belfast in July (ten months from now) which would cost him £590. He estimates he would need £500 spending money as well. Do you think James can afford to go on this holiday? Justify your answer.

Offers of credit are readily available today, but credit always has to be repaid.

Needs and wants

We all have needs and wants. Needs are things which are necessary (e.g., somewhere to live, food and clothes); wants are what we would like to have.

◆ We need clothes: we want designer jeans, shirts of different colours or a number of pairs of shoes.

◆ We need food: we could live on a very restricted diet but we want variety in what we eat.

With the influence of advertising and television our wants today are very extensive. In fact, they are almost limitless. Unfortunately we cannot have all that we want. We are restricted by what we can afford to buy.

Our income can be supplemented by obtaining credit through the use of credit cards, bank loans or overdrafts. These all, however, carry credit limits which are set by the provider of the finance according to our income and commitments. The amount we can borrow is restricted to our ability to repay. Even with borrowing we have a limit to what we can spend; we are still restricted by what we can afford to buy.

Everyone's decision about their spending relates to their 'lifestyle choices'. More and more people are nowadays choosing not to worry about promotion and making money because they prefer less pressure and a more relaxed lifestyle.

Opportunity cost

When your money is restricted you have to make choices: you may want a bar of chocolate and a can of fizzy drink but if you only have enough money for one or the other, you have to choose which to buy. If you decide to buy the chocolate, the drink becomes the **opportunity cost** of the chocolate.

Opportunity cost is the item you have to do without in order to buy the item you want. It is your lost opportunity. Likewise, within a family, the mum may want a new car, the dad may want a holiday and the children may want a new computer. There are limited funds available. If the mum gets the new car, the opportunity cost of this is the holiday and the computer.

activities

Imagine that your grandparents have just given you a cheque for £100 for your birthday.

1. Make a list of five items you want and place them in order of preference.

2. Use the Internet, newspapers or catalogues, or visit shops to find definite prices for these five items.

3. Indicate which of these items you are able to buy and give the opportunity cost of buying them.

Organisations' choices

Organisations such as schools and hospitals must budget in order to balance their finances.

Income dictates spending

Just like individuals or families, organisations (e.g., schools, libraries, hospitals and charities) have incomes and commitments. For example, schools receive their income from the government through their local education and library board. This income is allocated to the school to meet the educational requirements of the children enrolled. It has to be decided:

◆ how many staff are required

◆ what new books and stationery are needed

◆ what equipment has to be updated or replaced

◆ how much items such as rates, electricity, building maintenance and heating will cost.

All these costs of running a school are added up. The estimated expenditure is then offset against the income. If the estimated expenditure is higher than the income, decisions have to be made as to which items must be eliminated or reduced.

A school, just like an individual, is restricted in the amount it has to spend. The Board of Governors, which is responsible for the school budget, will have to consider staffing levels and the amounts being allocated to each area within the school. If the Governors decide that the level of teaching staff cannot be reduced other items of expenditure have to be considered in order to make the budget balance. It is then necessary to reduce the expenditure in other areas. This may mean, for example, that the opportunity cost of the expenditure needed for a teacher may be ten computers.

In addition to ensuring that expenditure is restricted to the available income, organisations also have the responsibility of ensuring that they get the most value for the amount of money spent. They must also strive to give the best possible service.

Difficult choices have to be made, as income and expenditure must balance!

The Manor Hospital Trust

The Manor Hospital Trust is responsible for the running of the Manor Regional Hospital. As a hospital trust it must keep to an allocated budget and ensure that the best value is obtained for money spent. It must also ensure that government targets are met with regard to patients. The Manor Hospital Trust tries to maintain or improve staffing levels and obtain the most up-to-date equipment. It is restricted at times by the amount of money available within its budget.

The outpatients department in the hospital is currently trying to improve the use of its allocation within the hospital budget.

Recently this notice was displayed in the outpatients' department:

> Have you had difficulty getting an appointment?
>
> Last month 705 patients failed to keep their appointment and did not notify the hospital
>
> This cost The Manor Hospital Trust £30,315
>
> If you cannot attend please telephone to cancel as your appointment can be given to someone who is in need of urgent care
>
> Thank You

These are considered fairly normal figures for an outpatients' clinic. As a consequence of this, the hospital tends to overbook clinics. Unfortunately, when all patients *do* turn up for appointments this causes problems because then the clinic runs late, patients become disgruntled and the government target of no more than 30 minutes' waiting time is not met.

At present, a patient is sent his/her appointment time by post when the hospital receives a referral from their GP. This appointment may be made six months in advance. Consideration is now being given to a partial booking system where the hospital will write to the patient, requesting the patient to contact them by phone to make an appointment. The appointment is therefore made for a time which is suitable for the patient.

A study of non-attendance at outpatients' clinics has highlighted that non-attendance at evening clinics is not as high as for daytime clinics.

When a patient does not turn up for an appointment, the hospital informs the GP of this but recognises that the GP will not necessarily have time to deal with this problem.

activity

Working in a group, discuss the problems being faced by this hospital trust and prepare a presentation of how you would rectify the problem using the information you have been given and your own suggestions.

Businesses' choices

A business exists to make profit. All business owners want to be successful. In order to be successful decisions have to be made by those running the business. With unlimited funds most businesses with good management could be successful. Managers would be able to decide how to improve or expand the business without having any financial restraints. Unfortunately, this is not the case for the vast majority of businesses. Businesses have to take into consideration financial constraints when making choices.

Businesses raise finances in many different ways. They may:

◆ keep profits in the business rather than paying them out to the owners

◆ bring in other owners who will pay capital into the business

◆ borrow money for the business from the owner or a member of the owner's family

◆ seek finance from outside financial organisations

◆ apply for a grant from the government.

Making choices

Just like individuals, businesses are limited in the amount of finance they can raise. This means that, in all businesses, choices have to be made in terms of expenditure. In a small engineering firm, replacing outdated machinery in the workshop might be considered to be more important than installing a new computer system. Likewise, a garage owner might decide to install a sandwich/hot food counter instead of a carwash. A business owner might also decide to replace employees with machinery if he/she feels that the **capital cost** of the machinery will, in the long term, be less than the ongoing costs of keeping employees.

The main considerations in making these decisions are cost, availability of the finance and the return on the investment to the business.

As future workers we need to be aware that all organisations operate within financial constraints. For example, financial constraints can affect possible career progression and restrict your opportunities for lifelong professional development.

Different sizes of businesses have different costs and financial restraints.

A leading clothing firm is to close its last manufacturing plant in Northern Ireland with the loss of nearly 300 jobs

DESMOND & SONS announced on Wednesday that it was closing its factory at Newbuildings, near Londonderry, where 277 jobs will be lost.

A cutting room at Springtown, Derry, where 16 people are employed, will also shut down.

In a statement issued on Wednesday, the company blamed 'significant competitive pressures' for its decision.

'Pressures on **margins**, coupled with increased insurance, energy and **social costs** combine to pose immense challenges to Northern Ireland manufacturing,' the company said.

'Despite our efforts to maintain as much employment locally as possible, the inevitable result of all these pressures is that products cease to be viable when made in Northern Ireland and must be produced overseas.

'Our competitors have long since ceased to manufacture garments in the UK.

'The decision to end all manufacturing locally is one that we made reluctantly, but we had no other option left open to us.

'Desmond's recognises the human consequences of such decisions and the sense of shock there will be, particularly at Newbuildings and at Springtown.'

Alan Elliot from the GMB union, which represents workers at the factory, said the government was also to blame for the job losses.

'Our government is sitting back watching their workers being put out of work,' he said.

'The jobs that are here are going overseas and they are doing nothing about it.'

Source: news.bbc.co.uk, 12 November 2003 (adapted)

activities

1. First, read the newspaper article above. Then, in your own words, list the reasons Desmond's gave for closing the plant.

2. Do you think this was an easy decision for Desmond's to make? Give reasons for your answer.

3. The Newbuildings plant made jeans for Marks & Spencer. A leading local economic correspondent has said that if Desmond's had been making jeans for a designer label such as Gucci, the plant, in all probability, would not have had to close. Why do you think this could be the case?

4. As a group, discuss the effects of this closure on the employees, other businesses in the area, and Northern Ireland in general.

The government's choices

Budgeting for all

The government has to provide for its citizens and necessary structures and services to keep the country operating properly (e.g., roads, railways, electricity, defence, education, health, etc.). It has to be committed to financing all public services that already exist, and to expanding and improving these services. Many employees are required in order to do this.

Chancellor Gordon Brown on his way to deliver his budget speech.

Each year, the Chancellor of the Exchequer – the government minister in charge of the country's finances – delivers a budget speech to the House of Commons. In this speech, the Chancellor gives details of how much he intends to spend in the coming year and how this money will be raised for the Exchequer.

In preparing for this speech, the Chancellor's department will have received estimates of expenditure for the next year from each government department. These estimates will have been prepared within the allocation made to the department. While a large part of each department's allocation is required to cover employee costs, choices still have to be made about how the remaining money is spent. Each department has to make choices about how the money is spent. For example, if the Department of Transport allocates money to a major motorway extension, the opportunity cost of this may be the building of a new flyover to alleviate congestion at a major intersection.

Government decisions can affect where there might be a growth in job opportunities. For example, the location of a new regional hospital or the construction of a new motorway will provide job opportunities in the designated areas. On the other hand, a decline in job opportunities is also possible, through the introduction of new technology or the closure of small local hospitals. The government's decisions, therefore, impact on where new job opportunities may arise. This will be one factor that may influence your career decision-making process!

Getting income

The government receives its income from taxes. It receives direct taxes, such as income tax and corporation tax from individuals and businesses, and indirect taxes on goods and services we buy (e.g., VAT – currently at 17.5 per cent – and duty on petrol).

The expenditure for running the country has to be balanced against the income which is received. When extra income is required, taxes are sometimes increased in the budget. The government could increase taxes to a very high rate in order to finance its plans (e.g., building new hospitals or schools, or developing new transport systems). However, large increases in taxes would not be popular with either individuals or businesses, so the government would lose support from the public and, eventually, would be voted out of office.

NO, I CAN'T GET RID OF TEACHERS AND PROVIDE EACH CHILD WITH A LAPTOP!

EDUCATION BUDGET

Government ministers must budget carefully to provide the required level of service.

As the government wants to remain popular and in office, tax increases are restricted to amounts which will generally be acceptable to the public. This means that a government cannot do everything it would like to improve the quality of life of its citizens and increase its popularity. So, governments, like individuals, businesses and organisations, have to operate under financial constraints.

Within Northern Ireland the Minister of Finance prepares the local budget, allocating an amount to each department in the Northern Ireland Assembly.

activities

Before starting these activities it may be helpful to obtain at least two different editions of a Northern Ireland newspaper giving public service job opportunities. Your teacher will be able to direct you to the relevant publications.

Below are the proposed public expenditure plans for Northern Ireland for 2004–2005:

Public Expenditure Plans: 2004–2005

Department	2003–2004 £m	2004–2005 £m	%
Agriculture and Rural Development	253.8	259.0	2.0
Culture, Arts and Leisure	97.1	101.6	4.6
Education	1,539.0	1,661.7	8.0
Employment and Learning	680.7	689.2	1.2
Enterprise, Trade and Investment	251.6	266.0	5.7
Finance and Personnel	165.7	174.2	5.1
Health, Social Services and Public Safety	3,041.1	3,247.8	6.8
Environment	133.2	141.3	6.1
Regional Development	609.3	684.1	12.3
Social Development	473.3	519.8	9.8
Office of First Minister and Deputy First Minister	49.2	53.1	7.9
Northern Ireland Assembly	49.2	49.2	0.0
Other departments	7.9	8.3	4.7

Source: Department of Finance and Personnel website (adapted)

1. Study the table above and list the departments in which there may possibly be a growth in job opportunities in 2004–2005. Give reasons for your choices.

2. Using your local newspapers, find job advertisements that are connected to some of the government departments in the table. Which government department has advertised the most job opportunities? Do you think there could be any connections between the time of year and the number of job opportunities available?

3. Can you find evidence of a higher salary and better qualifications being attached to career progression in any of the advertisements? Give details.

4. Select three departments and, using your local newspapers and resources in your school careers centre, find at least five job advertisements that will be funded by your chosen government departments. An example would be an advertisement for a doctor which would be funded by the department of Health, Social Services and Public Safety.

Introduction

In recent years the world of work has changed in a number of ways. The introduction of new technologies has brought about changes in the ways people work, the shift from industrial manufacturing to service provision has created different types of jobs and the end of 'jobs for life' has created a need for **lifelong learning** and increased skills levels. This section looks at the key **transferable skills** employers are looking for and the reasons why it is important to continue learning new skills throughout your life. It also looks at how to plan your career and how to apply for a job.

4. Key transferable skills

This unit clarifies a number of key transferable skills. The explanations will help you reflect on your skills and the importance of developing such skills throughout your career.

There is no definitive list of key transferable skills. They are simply skills learned in one context that are useful in another. They are a set of skills that can be applied to many different tasks, and that individuals need in order to be effective in an adaptable and competitive workforce. They are skills that people can continue to develop throughout their lifelong learning (see page 28–29).

Employers seek workers that have a range of key transferable skills. They want employees who have the ability to work amicably and productively with others, who can use technology, manage resources and use information effectively.

Key transferable skills that employers are looking for can fall into the following categories:

Essential skills

Reading, writing, listening and speaking are often referred to as essential skills. As Information Technology is being introduced at an early age to all young people in school, it could now also be seen as a necessary essential skill.

Critical and creative skills

Increasingly, employers are placing more and more emphasis on skills that could fall into the category of critical and creative skills. These could include:

- decision-making
- problem-solving
- being aware of costs
- efficient use of time
- customer service skills
- being able to set goals and meet targets
- visualisation (the ability to see an overall picture of what you want to achieve)
- **creative thinking** (the ability to come up with a different/new way of approaching a task)
- being innovative (having an idea that has not been developed before).

Personal and interpersonal skills

Personal and **interpersonal skills** include being able to:

- take responsibility
- demonstrate commitment, drive, enthusiasm, motivation, assertiveness and resourcefulness
- receive feedback
- working well with others
- displaying leadership, negotiation, communication, persuasion and influence skills
- giving feedback
- sensitivity
- being able to delegate
- encouraging others.

1. Rewrite the speech bubbles for the cartoons (right):

   ◆ For cartoon 1) write a speech bubble showing what you consider to be good customer service skills.

   ◆ For cartoon 2) write a speech bubble that would provide feedback in a sensitive way.

2. What do you know about your own transferable skills? Copy and complete this table. (Keep a copy of your answers to this task as it would be interesting to complete it again next term/year to see if there are any changes to your answers.)

1)  **2)**

What skills are these people lacking?

Skills	Have you learned this skill? (Yes/No)	Do you need to develop this skill? (Yes/No)	Comments
Making a commitment and sticking to it			
Working with people you don't necessarily like			
Patience			
Discipline			
Respect			
Creativity			
Ability to take orders			
Self-control			
Communication skills			
Drive and dedication (the ability to push yourself to the limit)			
Knowing your limitations			
Ability to accept complete responsibility for your behaviour			
Ability to accept criticism and feedback in order to learn			
Risk-taking			
Ability to evaluate yourself			
Flexibility			
Ability to perform under pressure			

3. Consider a job that you are interested in. Find out about the job using the following headings as a guide:

   ◆ job title

   ◆ job description

   ◆ qualifications needed

   ◆ hours of work

   ◆ main skills required to do the job.

Now write a report using the headings as your structure and present your findings to the class.

You could find the information you need by:

   ◆ talking to someone already doing this job

   ◆ researching information at the careers reference library at your school

   ◆ searching websites

   ◆ using the Odyssey careers software.

Your teacher might want to use this task as part of your assessment for presentation.

Providing Quality Education and Training for Life

Part-time Prospectus 2003/04

nei
North East Institute of
Further & Higher Education
Associate College of the University of Ulster

www.neifac.uk

A leaflet advertising further education from the North East Institute of Further & Higher Education.

This unit outlines the reasons why you would want, or need, to continue learning throughout your life and how you can go about this.

Reasons for lifelong learning

Within the context of work, it is necessary to continue to develop existing skills and acquire new skills, along with qualifications, as the world of work continues to change.

In unit 1 you discovered how many products and services are being imported from other countries where wages are lower and, therefore, where it is cheaper to have goods manufactured. This has an effect on the jobs available and the skills required for those jobs. You will discover as you grow older that there will be periods when certain sectors of industry and employment have more job vacancies than others; such shifts in employment opportunities are generally temporary.

Continuing learning

There are a number of ways of finding out about opportunities to continue learning new skills and take further qualifications after you have left full-time education. A few are listed below.

Institutes of further and higher education

These institutes not only offer full-time study courses during the day, but they also offer a wide range of courses for people who want to study part-time (e.g., studying for one day a week while they are in employment and are sponsored by their employer, or studying through courses that are available in the evening for a qualification that can be gained over a period of one or two years).

LearnDirect

These are centres that offer training in a wide range of job areas, for people who wish to continue to update their skills. They also have an Internet-based information, advice and guidance service for learning and employment, which can be found at www.learndirect-futures.co.uk

Job centres

Job centres not only advertise jobs that are available in your area, but careers office advisers are there to give guidance and advice on how best to update your skills and portfolio. They also have a vast knowledge of training that would be available to you.

EGSA (Educational Guidance Service for Adults)

This is a local, independent organisation that aims to connect adults with learning services and is free to individuals. They have offices all over Northern Ireland and are based in Ballymoney, Belfast, Craigavon, Londonderry, Dungannon, Larne, Magherafelt, Newry and Omagh. They work closely with LearnDirect and, through their resources, can provide information on adult learning provision across Northern Ireland, Republic of Ireland, Great Britain and on distance learning. As well as a research library, they can advise on funding for courses and provide information on events that are taking place (e.g., seminars and events such as Adult Learning Week). Their website is www.egsa.org.uk

activities

Read the case study below. Imagine that you are working in the local job centre as a careers adviser, and that both John and Patricia have arranged a meeting with you.

1. Prepare for their visit by researching all the routes that might be open to them.
2. Present your findings in a word-processed document ready for the interview.

CASE STUDY

John and Patricia

John and Patricia now need to change direction.

John and his wife Patricia had been employed in their local shirt factory for all of their working life, so it came as a shock for them both when they lost their jobs a few months ago when the factory closed down. John is 35 years old and his wife is 29 years old. Their two children are both at school so both John and Patricia want and need to work full-time. John left school with seven GCSEs, with grades ranging from A to D. He went into an engineering apprentice programme at 16 with his present employer. He managed the installation of a complete plant of machinery a number of years ago.

Patricia also left school and went to work in the factory. She has five GCSEs, but was not interested in continuing in education, as the factory work was paying very good wages. Now she regrets this decision and wants to look in a different direction to obtain a full-time job. She was responsible for quality-checking the garments as they came off the production line.

6. The career planning process

This unit aims to explain how career planning is a continuous lifelong process that will help you assess and review your own skills, qualities and aptitudes, explore career pathways and equip you with research skills to help manage your career.

The career planning process involves four stages:

1. **Review**. This is when you examine the situation at the present time, in order to decide how to move forward.

2. **Goal-setting**. This is when you decide an outcome which you will then work towards.

3. **Target-setting**. This is the process of breaking the goal up into manageable steps so that each step becomes a SMART target:

   S Specific
   M Manageable
   A Achievable
   R Realistic
   T Time-bound

4. **Action**. This is when you consider each target and decide what action is required in order to achieve the outcome you desire.

A model of the planning process

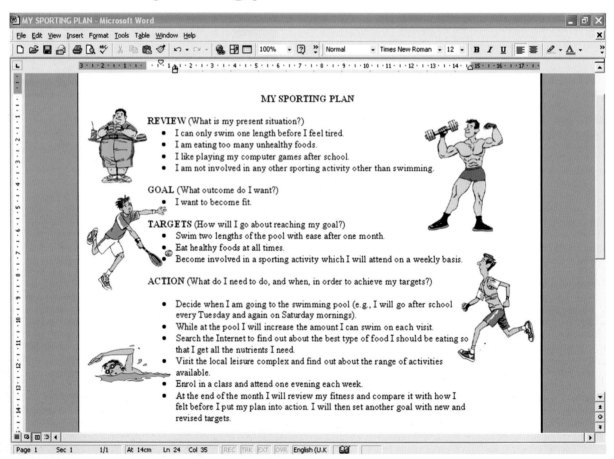

The planning process can be applied to many situations.

Your career plan

The plan on page 30 is a cyclical process. This means that the four stages will be repeated again, as you might reconsider your fitness at different stages of your life, both in school and throughout your life. The following diagram demonstrates how the same process can be applied to career planning.

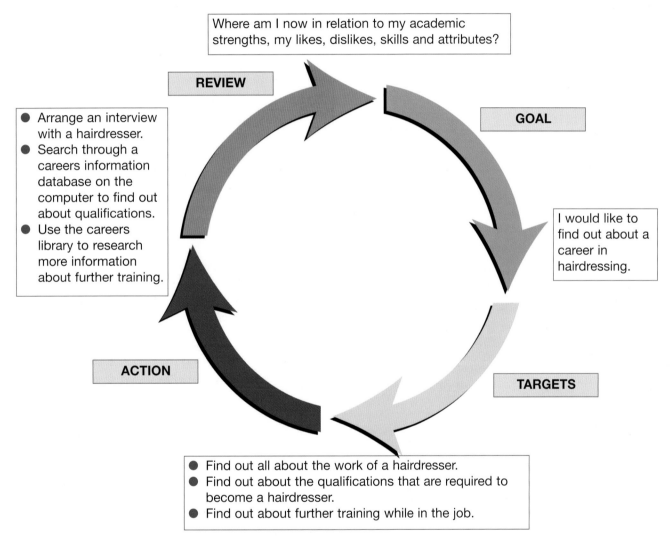

REVIEW

Where am I now in relation to my academic strengths, my likes, dislikes, skills and attributes?

GOAL

I would like to find out about a career in hairdressing.

- Arrange an interview with a hairdresser.
- Search through a careers information database on the computer to find out about qualifications.
- Use the careers library to research more information about further training.

ACTION

TARGETS

- Find out all about the work of a hairdresser.
- Find out about the qualifications that are required to become a hairdresser.
- Find out about further training while in the job.

If you were carrying out the actions as outlined in the diagram above, you would next analyse the information collected and review what you thought about a career in hairdressing. You would compare the skills, qualities and qualifications required with what you know about yourself. This would then help you set a new goal with new targets. You might conclude that hairdressing would not be a suitable career and decide to investigate another area. This type of career plan can be used for any type of job you are interested in.

activity

Imagine that you want to buy a new portable CD player. This is your goal. Draw up a plan to include the four stages, stating clearly what you would do at each stage in order to achieve your goal.

Career exploration

Personal career planning is a process that is used to enable you to identify each stage of your preferred options. Your plan will constantly be updated in the light of your research and experiences that you engage in as you go through life.

In order for you to be able to identify your preferred options, you need to be able to research, analyse and evaluate information about different careers and the career paths open to you.

Sources of information

Careers information comes in many forms:

◆ books

◆ magazines

◆ brochures

◆ leaflets

◆ videos

◆ software

◆ college and university prospectuses

◆ trade directories

◆ posters

◆ Internet sites.

Career notes can be downloaded from www.gov.uk. They provide information on various careers.

activity

Jamie, a new student, has joined your class. You have been asked by the teacher to prepare a leaflet for Jamie, which would give him information about the different resources that are in the careers library in your school.

You will need to visit the careers library and carry out some research for the preparation of your leaflet.

Below are some ideas about the type of information that you would want to include for Jamie.

◆ Find out the name of a software programme used by the careers library and explain its purpose

◆ Give the title of a book that would help with making decisions about career planning. Write a brief summary of what the book is about

◆ Find out about a university prospectus and give details of how it can be located in the library

◆ Explain to Jamie where he can find a leaflet about modern apprenticeships.

The Internet is a useful source of information.

The qualifications framework

When you begin to research information about jobs that interest you, you will find out about the qualifications that are required to do that particular job. Talk to your careers teacher for more details about this.

GCSE

The General Certificate of Secondary Education (GCSE) is a means of assessing what you have attained at the end of your compulsory secondary education, at the end of Key Stage 4.

GCSEs in vocational subjects

These GCSE qualifications introduce you to a broad sector of industry and business and encourage understanding of this area. They also give you the opportunity to develop the skills that are required in industry and business (e.g., dealing with the general public). They are designed to provide you with the opportunity to explore areas in an innovative way through research, and help you to develop entrepreneurial skills within a vocational context (such as construction, engineering, journalism). They provide the same standards as the traditional GCSEs.

GCE AS-level

The AS-level qualification represents the first half of the full A-level and is designed to enable you to study a wider range of subjects in the first year of post-16 work. Most AS-level subjects have three assessment units. These units contribute to full A-levels, which have six assessment units. The AS-level is a qualification in its own right. Coursework can contribute to the result. The AS-level is graded from A to E.

GCE A-level: A2

The second year of the full A-level is called A2. The full A-level is normally made up of six assessment units (this includes the three AS-level assessment units) taken either over two years (modular) or as a set of exams at the end of two years (linear).

A2 modules do not make up a qualification in their own right. Coursework can contribute to the result. There is a coursework limit with a ceiling of 30 per cent in most A-level subjects. A2s are graded from A to E.

Vocational Certificate of Education (VCEs)

The Vocational Certificate of Education replaced GNVQs. They are graded from A to E to show that they are comparable to GCE A-levels.

These emphasise knowledge, skills and understanding in broad vocational areas and focus on investigative work and assignment writing. They also foster links with employers and concentrate on working as part of a team. Two-thirds of the work is internally assessed and externally moderated.

The basic qualification is the six-unit vocational A-level, equivalent to one GCE A-level. There is also a 12-unit double award, equivalent to two A-levels and a three-unit award in a limited number of subjects.

NVQs

National Vocational Qualifications develop the skills, knowledge and understanding needed in specific jobs (e.g., hairdressing, plumbing). They are competence-based and operate at five levels.

Modern apprenticeships

Modern apprenticeship is a popular route to gain further qualifications.

Modern apprenticeships are a pathway into employment and training for people between the ages of 16 and 21. You are paid to learn from experts for two to four years, depending on the industry you choose. As a modern apprentice you are assigned your own personal mentor whose job it is to help you succeed. A personal training plan is tailored to your needs and progress is regularly reviewed against the training plan. Modern apprenticeship training leads to an NVQ. Modern apprenticeships are popular in the fields of engineering, electrical work and construction.

activities

Do you know your careers resources? How good is your job analysis?

1. Choose a career of your choice that you want to find out more about. Use at least three sources of information for your research (e.g., software, videos, leaflets).

2. Copy and complete the resources worksheet opposite.

3. Using the job analysis framework below, select the appropriate information from your research findings and prepare a short presentation for your class.

Job analysis framework

The work

What does the job involve?
Where does it take place?
What other people are involved?
What are the hours?

Skills and interests

What interests would help you do this job?
What skills would you need?

Qualifications

What qualifications, if any, are required for entry into this job?

Levels of entry

Are there a number of different entry routes you can take to become eligible to do this job?

School subjects

What school subjects would be suitable to take for this job?

Training opportunities and prospects

Can you get training on the job?
Is there an opportunity to gain further qualifications for this job?

RESOURCES CHECKLIST

Job researched:_____

What resources are available for use in the careers room?		List of resources to be used: _____ _____ _____
Are any of my friends, family or neighbours involved with this job?		If yes, I will make contact by: _____ _____ _____
Are any local businesses offering this type of work?		List of businesses to be consulted: _____ _____ _____
What other outside agencies could provide information?		List of agencies: _____ _____ _____
How will my final information be presented?		Explain: _____ _____ _____

7. The job application process

Changing patterns of work

Because of the radical transformations worldwide in both the nature and the patterns of work, it has become increasingly important to be able to communicate your talents and express your creative abilities in order to compete for jobs in the marketplace. We all have different:

- capacities (that is the gift to do different things)
- aptitudes (the ability to acquire particular skills)
- biographies (different experiences both inside and outside school).

We have different pasts and will have different futures.

The career planning process that you have been engaging in will help you to understand your past and help you to find your future. You have already discovered your own strengths, likes and dislikes, and you need to continually reflect and build upon the positive aspects of your character.

This unit provides an overview of the job application process and takes you through writing your **curriculum vitae** and completing an application form.

Curriculum vitaes

Compiling a curriculum vitae (CV) is one way of building a personal profile. It is a personally designed document that sets out the main details about yourself (e.g., name, address, age, qualifications, experience, hobbies/interests, names and addresses of referees).

activities

1. Think back to when you began attending this school and list all the clubs and after-school activities that you have taken part in. You might also want to include activities that you are involved in outside school. Then write down:
   - whether each activity/club involved working with other people as part of a team (e.g., school choir, netball team)
   - whether you had the opportunity at any time to lead the team in any event
   - the skills that you developed while taking part in the activity.
2. List any part-time jobs you may have had and/or any voluntary work you have done and note the skills that you developed while taking part in this type of work.

By completing the above activity you are building up a portfolio of evidence that shows an employer the type of person you are and the skills that you have already been developing. As you mature it is important that you continue to record the strengths you have and evidence of how you apply the skills that make you employable.

How do these photos show changing patterns of work?

Curriculum Vitae

NAME   Oliver TWIST

TELEPHONE   0714 9219

ADDRESS   Gads Hill Place
Rochester Road
Nr Gravesend
Kent GR3 4PD

DATE OF BIRTH   23.12.1839

EDUCATION
School Board Academy
Workhouse Lane
Irchester
Northamptonshire

QUALIFICATIONS

GCSE		
	Maths	Grade C
	English Language	Grade A
	English Literature	Grade C
	Physics	Grade D
	CDT	Grade B
	Oakum picking	Grade D
	Geography	Grade C

OTHER QUALIFICATIONS
Duke of Edinburgh's Bronze Award (70-mile expedition, personal survival, casualty simulation)

WORK EXPERIENCE
Apprentice mute (three weeks)
Sowerbury Funeral Service
Rushden
Northants

Street collection work (two weeks)
Fagin and Associates
Field Lane
London E12

INTERESTS
My main interests are food appreciation and cross-country running. I also perform in the annual musical production of the local dramatic society.

REFEREES
Mr C Brownlow (Retired book dealer)
17 Providence Row
Pentonville Road
London N1

Mr William Sykes (House clearance consultant)
Farthing Alley
London SE1

Example of a CV from CCEA Preparing for Work Experience.

Job recruitment

If you are already in a job, you could change your role within the same company by applying for a position that may be advertised internally. This means that the firm advertises the job within the business only.

Businesses recruit from outside through:

◆ newspaper and magazine advertisements

◆ job centres, which are run by the Department of Employment and Learning, and are found in major towns. They display jobs on cards either in the window or inside the building on noticeboards

◆ Private employment agencies that help businesses to recruit staff (e.g., secretarial workers, nurses and teachers).

Some jobs may only attract a few applicants. If the job is unskilled, the company may interview immediately those people who ring up or call in. For the majority of jobs there will be a formal procedure. On receipt of the job description which sets out what the person appointed to the job will have to do, you will be asked to complete either a CV or an application form. The application form asks for information that would normally be contained in a CV.

Before completing an application form, it is a good idea to think about your personal qualities and how they demonstrate the skills that the job advertised is looking for. Remember, this is your opportunity to get into the next round: the interview. You are often asked to write a covering letter to go with your CV. You should adapt your CV to reflect evidence of the skills the job is asking for. If the job you are applying for is a trainee management post, then you should emphasise your skills of leadership. You might find evidence of your development of these skills, for example, if you were captain of a team at school. An example of an application form can be found on page 39.

An example of an application form can be found on page 39.

activity

Word-process your CV in response to one of the adverts (below) for part-time jobs that have been advertised in a local shop window. You should:

◆ make sure that you include all relevant information

◆ make sure that your referees are able and willing to be contacted by the employer

◆ check all spelling carefully, along with correct names, addresses and dates

◆ spend time drafting and proofreading

◆ take care with the presentation of your CV.

WANTED

URGENTLY REQUIRED

Person willing to do paper round 2 evenings per week

Apply by sending CV to:
The Manager, Wayside Stores,
Longfield, Ballyhulbert

WAITER/WAITRESS
URGENTLY REQUIRED

Person willing to serve in busy restaurant
Friday and Saturday evenings.
Hours: 5.30–9.30 pm

Hourly rates of pay apply.

Send CV to:
The Restaurant Manager,
Calypso's restaurant,
14 Pound Street, Marketdene

c/o BP Oil UK Ltd
Airport Road West
Belfast BT3 9EA
Telephone 01 232 739639
Facsimile 01 232 461471
E-mail: info@bitc.org.uk

Banbridge Enterprise Centre
Scarva Road Industrial Estate
Banbridge BT32 3QD
Telephone 018206 25892
Facsimile 018206 22264

Chamber of Commerce House
1, St. Columb's Court, Bishop Street
Londonderry BT48 6PT
Telephone 01504 365786
Facsimile 01504 374683

APPLICATION FOR EMPLOYMENT

PLEASE PRINT CLEARLY IN BLACK INK. USE ADDITIONAL SHEETS IF NECESSARY.

POSITION APPLIED FOR: _____ REF: _____

PERSONAL

Surname	Title	Forenames
Address (in full)		Telephone numbers Private Business

Is there any reason why you would not be able to
perform any aspects of this job? YES/NO

_____

We have a policy of interviewing all disabled candidates
who meet the essential criteria.

Would you like to be considered under this policy? YES/NO

Do you have a current driving licence? YES/NO

Do you have access to a car for business use? YES/NO

When would you be available to start work?

 President: H.R.H. The Prince of Wales.
N. Ireland Chairman: Stephen Kingon. Regional Director: John Heaslip.
Registered office: 44 Baker Street, London W1M 1DH.
A limited company No. 1619253. Registered Charity No: 297716
Business in the Community is the leading authority on business involvement in the community INVESTOR IN PE

74

Interests

Additional Information

If you feel there is anything which has not been covered adequately elsewhere on your application form,
please elaborate below.

When would you be available if offered employment?

References

Give names, addresses, occupations and telephone numbers of two referees. Ideally one should be a
previous employer. These will not be contacted until you have been advised. (BLOCK LETTERS)

Declaration

I certify that all the information I have given is correct. I understand that any false information given may
result in any job offer being withdrawn.

Signed: Date:

73

A example of an application form

activities

1. Look at the following words:

> reliable capable dependable amiable
> sociable conscientious industrious
> meticulous ambitious

2. Check that you know the meaning of all of these words. Write a brief definition of each one.
3. Write a paragraph about yourself using some of the above words.

How do companies select employees?

Depending on the job, there can be a number of stages that you will have to go through. If you have applied for a hairdressing position in the local hairdressing salon, you would probably be called for an interview quite soon after sending a CV or on completion of an application form.

If you are applying for an apprenticeship you may have to complete a number of aptitude tests. These test your ability in areas related to the job (e.g., how well you can do mathematical calculations in your head, or how well you can use your hands to perform certain tasks like holding different tools).

Sometimes companies use assessment centres as part of the selection process where applicants are observed interacting with each other on a number of tasks, which will demonstrate their interpersonal skills. Candidates may also be asked to make a presentation on a given topic.

If you are successful at the selection stage, the interview is the time to make an impression.

First impressions

First impressions do count. Consider wearing appropriate clothes when attending an interview. Clothes that you would consider wearing to a disco (e.g., jeans and t-shirt for boys, and jeans and a top or short skirt, with lots of make-up, for girls) would not be considered suitable for an interview situation. Think smart, tidy and conservative (e.g., plain, dark trousers or skirt-suit for girls, and trousers, shirt, tie and jacket for boys).

Remember a firm handshake when you are introduced to your potential employer. Smile and answer questions with sentences, never 'yes' or 'no' only. You will be able to do this if you have prepared for your interview, and have found out as much as you can about the company and the job beforehand.

CASE STUDY

Joshua Rossenvale

Joshua Rossenvale is a geography graduate who has worked as a warden with the National Trust since he left university five years ago. His work involves showing tourists and groups of school children around properties owned and preserved by the National Trust. He enjoys presenting talks to both adult and student audiences.

He has also worked as a tourist guide for his local council during the holiday period while at university, and supplemented his student grant with work in the restaurant of a local hotel at weekends. In his spare time he attends his local gym and plays football for his town's team. A job has been advertised for a project officer to lead an environmental programme in the primary school sector; he has decided to complete an application form.

activity

Imagine you are Joshua and copy and complete the application form on page 39. Be creative here with the personal details and dates. Remember, handwriting, correct grammar and spelling are important. Joshua wants this job so he needs to sell himself.

Your behaviour during job interviews will really affect how successful you are.

activity

Which man in the pictures above (A or B) do you think is more likely to get the job? Give reasons for your answer.

Introduction

This section explores the meaning of enterprise and the skills associated with being enterprising, as well as looking at the characteristics of an entrepreneur and how these are used in running a business. It also examines the skills and qualities that we each have that enable us to be enterprising as individuals or as part of a group.

8. What is enterprise?

For many people 'enterprise' and 'entrepreneurship' are immediately associated with business. Entrepreneurship is connected to the running of a successful business and is an ability which may be developed, although few people possess it to a high degree. Enterprise, on the other hand, is an ability that we can all bring to our daily lives in many different ways: we can change our appearance, we can change our attitude to others and we can move in a different direction. We are all enterprising but we are not all **entrepreneurs.**

The term 'enterprise' is used in many different ways. The Oxford dictionary defines 'enterprise' as 'an undertaking, especially a bold or difficult one', while the Chambers dictionary defines it as 'an undertaking or a new project'. From these definitions we can understand that enterprise is an undertaking which is new, difficult or bold. It has been said that enterprise is difficult to define but easily recognised.

Many young people show enterprise by taking part in hikes, community service or by developing a new interest (e.g., as part of the Duke of Edinburgh Award

Challenge, excitement and risk for Ellen MacArthur in the Round the World Yacht Challenge.

Scheme). Others show enterprise when they become part of a group raising money for charity. Likewise, it is enterprising when young people design and build a robot to take part in a challenge or organise a youth club event (e.g., a disco or quiz).

To take part in a pop competition on national television, to climb Everest, to be blind and a water skiing champion, to walk the length of Ireland for a cancer charity: these can all be identified as being enterprising. But what makes people want to undertake such new projects? It may be because they developed a new interest, or needed the excitement of a new challenge, possibly involving some risk.

activity

List some of the things you have done in the last three years that you might identify as being enterprising for you. You may work in groups to do this or simply draw up your own list.

An idea

We are all enterprising at different times and in different ways, but all new projects have to start with an idea. Often we get ideas from watching television, reading newspapers or listening to others. An idea is something that is new or novel – something you haven't done before.

I've just thought of it!

Enterprising qualities

Having an idea is the crux of enterprise but it is only the beginning. Without other enterprising qualities the idea would remain just an idea. To be enterprising, a person has to:

◆ use his or her initiative to get going (take the first step to start a project)

◆ have a realistic goal (know and understand what is achievable with the finance and support available)

◆ draw up a plan of how to achieve this goal (have definite steps of progression from the start through to the conclusion of the project)

◆ know the sources of help and be prepared to listen to advice (find out what help is available and take on board the advice given)

◆ network by using contacts who could be helpful (make contact with and use those who are in a position to be able to provide help and support)

◆ be able to persuade others to help (convince other people that your idea is viable and gain their help)

◆ negotiate with others to get what is needed (confer and compromise with others to bring about what you need and want)

◆ be able to assess the risk involved (know and understand what is involved if the idea does not work)

◆ be prepared to see the project through (have the patience and endurance to stick with the project through the early problems and obstacles until success is achieved).

We can now say that a person has certain skills and attributes which make him or her enterprising. These enterprising qualities are summarised below:

innovativeness

networking

creativity

listening

initiative

negotiation

commitment

time and money management

vision

risk-taking

By using these skills and attributes and seeking out an opportunity, a person gets the rewards and satisfaction of being enterprising. Can you link each of these skills and attributes to at least one enterprising quality?

activity

Identify occasions when you have used the following enterprising qualities:

◆ negotiation
◆ networking
◆ initiative
◆ commitment
◆ time and money management.

43

Enterprise at work

Being enterprising in a work situation may be rewarding either as an employee or employer. Often an employee who is carrying out a task is the person to identify how a product, process or service can be changed for the better or how a new product could be introduced. Many employers encourage employees to be innovative by financially rewarding good and successful suggestions and ideas. This is to the advantage of both the employer and employee.

It happens, however, that when an employee has a really good idea (if he or she has developed other enterprising qualities) it is the **catalyst** that makes that person move forward to start up his or her own business – to become an entrepreneur.

In Northern Ireland there are over 84,000 businesses, most of which employ less than 50 people. Since there are few big employers, we need many more people to start their own businesses to strengthen our economy and make us less dependent on the **public sector** for employment. It is for this reason that the government has set up support agencies to help those who are considering starting their own business.

Department of Enterprise, Trade and Investment (DETI)

This is the government department responsible for promoting and supporting enterprise, trade and investment, both within Northern Ireland and for Northern Ireland businesses trading globally.

Invest Northern Ireland

This is an economic development agency. It operates in the context of the overall policy set by the DETI. It aims to harness the educational, cultural and environmental strengths of Northern Ireland by encouraging innovation and entrepreneurship to create an environment in which businesses – whether local or from overseas – will flourish. It provides support to existing businesses in order that they remain competitive in global markets. This help and support takes many forms; for example, it promotes Northern Ireland's goods and services at trade fairs both at home and abroad, and provides training and support for business initiatives such as electronic communications. It also offers a range of support to people thinking of starting up a new business through the enterprise agency network known as Enterprise Northern Ireland.

Enterprise Northern Ireland

This has a network of local enterprise agencies that support small businesses and community enterprises by providing guidance on grants and initiatives available to small businesses. It also provides professional advice from experienced business people as well as programmes to help and support businesses to grow and develop. Expert advice is available on low-cost loans, how to obtain any financial help that may be available in your particular area and other business finance. Industrial and office accommodation may also be provided, together with support for businesses acquiring new technologies.

Guidance and support is available for entrepreneurs.

Shell LiveWIRE finalists 2003.

Shell LiveWIRE

Shell LiveWIRE is partly funded by Shell. It promotes starting a business as a valid career to young people aged 16–30, providing advice, support and guidance. It also runs the Young Entrepreneur of the Year Award that provides a promotional opportunity for young people who have just started in business, as well as very worthwhile prizes.

Prince's Trust

If you are aged 18–30, unemployed or in a part-time or inadequate job, and have an idea for a business but can't raise all the cash you need from anywhere else, the Prince's Trust could help you. It provides low-interest loans or grants as well as offering specialist and ongoing advice from a volunteer business person.

activity

Identify which of the agencies on pages 44–45 would be best placed to help and support

- a young unemployed person with an idea for a business
- your school group studying for GCSE Learning for Life and Work
- a bed and breakfast business wishing to set up a website and take online bookings
- an American manufacturer of electronic equipment seeking a base in Europe
- a Northern Irish designer and manufacturer of specialist sportwear who has developed a range of surfwear. The UK and Ireland are her current market, but she would like to expand further.

Social enterprise

Some people use their enterprise skills for the good of the community. This is often called social enterprise. These people identify a local 'need' (e.g., the need for a play area for children, a drop-in centre for young adults or a learning centre for the unemployed). Having identified the need they then proceed to network with key influencers, such as the local MP, members of the local council, or local business people. This will enable them to persuade and sell their idea. Gaining support from local politicians and businesses will generate greater publicity for their scheme and help to raise the necessary funds through a higher profile.

Kilcronaghan Activity and Conference Centre.

CASE STUDY

Kilcronaghan Activity and Conference Centre

Kilcronaghan Activity and Conference Centre is the brainchild of Kilcronaghan Community Association (KCA), a group of local people whose aim is to support and help the local community.

◆ It is situated at the foot of the Sperrin mountains in the Magherafelt district (a popular area for walkers).

◆ It has ensuite accommodation for up to 34 residents at keen prices, as well as large common rooms which may be used by groups or organisations for teambuilding, training or conference purposes.

◆ It is close to the 'Porter's Pit' track at Desertmartin. This is a popular venue for Moto X riders and fans from all over Ireland and further afield.

◆ The centre is popular for children's birthday parties.

◆ Conference facilities are available for local business and community groups.

◆ Schools in the area use the accommodation for exchange students.

◆ Schools and youth clubs use the centre for residential visits.

◆ Much of the work within the centre is done on a voluntary basis.

◆ In opening this centre, KCA enabled an old church rectory to be restored and retained as part of the local community.

activity

As a group, using the information in the case study (left), discuss why you think this centre is run by a community association to enhance the local community, and not by an entrepreneur as a business for profit.

Using enterprise

We should recognise that within our working lives we must try to be enterprising. This may be through simply finding an easier way to complete a task, or by considering within your personal career plan (see unit 7) an opportunity to diversify at some stage and move in a different direction. It may also be to plan to move from being an employee to becoming self-employed. Having an open mind and keeping options open makes it much easier to change and move in different directions. This will provide you with a greater number of opportunities to succeed.

Helping women to make leap of faith

The following is an extract from a newspaper article in which the co-ordinator of Women in Business answered a number of questions relating to the role of women in business.

What issues do women in business face that men don't?

Males are more than four times as likely to be self-employed than females in Northern Ireland. The self-employment rate is 4.2 per cent for women here, compared to 17.8 per cent for males (Labour Force Survey 2002). Northern Ireland is the second lowest of all UK regions for female self-employment rates.

The Latent Entrepreneurship Study (commissioned by Invest Northern Ireland with a sample of 5,500 individuals) questioned young people while in school about their ambitions. They then followed this up later to find out how many had fulfilled them. The study showed that one in three female sixth-formers expressed an interest in self-employment, but only one in 10 actually do it five years on. Northern Ireland has a problem of translating thinkers into doers.

On the other hand, in the United States, 28 per cent of all businesses are women-owned.

Source: Business section of *Belfast Telegraph*, 29 August, 2003

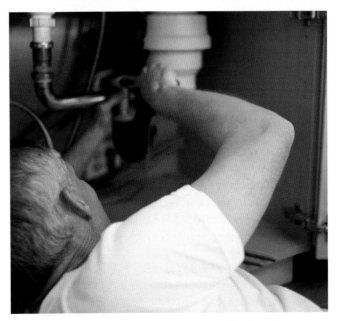

In Northern Ireland, men are more likely to be self-employed than women.

Idea + skills + attributes + qualities = enterprise

We have now looked at the skills, attributes and qualities which, together with the right idea, can make a person enterprising. He or she may be enterprising as a self-employed person in business, an employee, a person in the local community, or an individual increasing their personal achievements. You should now recognise the 'buzz' words and phrases attached to enterprise, such as 'idea', 'creativity' in pursuing an idea, 'networking' and using 'contacts', 'negotiation', 'persuasion' and 'selling' ourselves. From this we can now give a fuller definition of enterprise.

> **Enterprise is the ability of an individual or members of a group, using essential skills and attributes, to develop an original idea and bring it to a rewarding and successful conclusion.**

As a group, discuss what you think is preventing women in Northern Ireland from becoming self-employed.

9. Characteristics of an entrepreneur

A characteristic is a trait that is part of an individual. We all have traits in our character which make us individual. For example, we may be inquisitive, cautious, modest or lazy. Our character comprises of a number of different characteristics. Some people have a number of characteristics which collectively help them to become entrepreneurs. These include:

◆ being a 'doer' (being prepared to personally undertake the work involved – not being afraid of getting your hands dirty!)

◆ being focused (being able to totally concentrate on the matter in hand at a particular time regardless of what is happening elsewhere)

◆ being visionary (having the creativity to think of an idea and having the capacity to see an overall picture of what you want to achieve now and in the future)

◆ being committed (his or her business becomes a lifestyle rather than a career)

◆ being hardworking (able to be a committed worker until the task is completed, and not giving up even when things get tough)

◆ being an expert in your area (researching and learning as much as possible, not only about your product or service, but also about the business matters connected with running your business effectively)

◆ being responsible (facing up to the consequences of running a business, being fully aware of what is involved and not being afraid)

◆ being dedicated (not letting go of your vision or giving up, even when faced with apparently insurmountable difficulties).

Within Northern Ireland we now have many successful businesses, some of which employ many people and others that employ relatively few, or perhaps even none. Regardless of its size and complexity, each business started with an idea from one person. In order to turn that idea into a successful business, that person had to find within him or herself the character and strength to face up to the struggle and hardship of becoming an entrepreneur.

In order to become successful, an entrepreneur has to have the success of his or her business as a first priority. A desire to make millions will not create a successful business. Microsoft tycoon Bill Gates' mission statement was never 'to be the richest man in the world'. It was 'a PC on every desk and in every home'.

activity

Can you define at least four characteristics that you possess as an individual? These may be things such as being lazy, hardworking, reckless or responsible. Be honest and try to find the strengths and weaknesses within your character. How do you think you could improve your weaknesses?

Entrepreneurs in Northern Ireland

By identifying the characteristics of an entrepreneur in people, it becomes easier to understand how they are necessary in order to have a successful business venture. In order to do this we are going to look at some case studies of successful Northern Irish entrepreneurs.

activity

Can you identify characteristics of an entrepreneur in Paul and Jeanne Rankin (see opposite)? List these and explain how you think they are showing these characteristics.

Paul left his native Belfast in 1980 to travel the world. During his visit to Greece he met Jeanne from Winnipeg, Canada. They continued travelling, financing themselves by working as waiters and in restaurant kitchens. Cooking became their passion and they returned to London for full professional training. When they married they moved to America with Paul eventually being in charge of his own hotel kitchen. Around this time Paul began to develop his own recipes and style of presentation which evolved into his business idea.

In 1989 they returned to Belfast with their two children. Although this was a time when there was still unrest and disruption to business and life in Belfast they were determined to make their business idea a success. They bought a bankrupt restaurant in the city and, in 1991, opened it as Roscoff. Many hours of hard work and commitment to ideals and standards resulted in it being awarded the much coveted Michelin star in 1991 – the first to be awarded in Northern Ireland.

After the success of Roscoff, Paul and Jeanne presented two local cookery series called *Gourmet Ireland* and the *Rankin Challenge*. The writing of cookery books and the development of a food hamper business also accompanied the *Gourmet Ireland* series. Since then, Paul has had regular slots on *Masterchef* and *Ready, Steady, Cook* on national television and is recognised as one of the top chefs in the United Kingdom.

In 1999 they closed Roscoff, refitted the premises and opened them as Cayenne, a restaurant with a more informal feel. In addition to this, they now also have five café outlets where, as well as the usual coffee and cakes, they sell their own speciality bread. Recently, they have opened Rain City Café Grill – another informal restaurant. They continue their hamper business named after their *Gourmet Ireland* television series and have recently published another book.

The couple are also involved with the Rankin Selection of Irish Bread range with Irwin's Bakery. This is a range of six items including fruit soda and potato bread. The Rankins were involved in the development of the range which is sold under their **imagery**. This bread is made by Irwin's Bakery in Portadown and sold to the major supermarket chains for retail sale in Great Britain and Ireland.

Women in business

In unit 8 we looked at the problem women in Northern Ireland have in becoming entrepreneurs. While this is a major problem and one that needs to be rectified there is a small but successful band of women within Northern Ireland who are successful in business and who manage to combine family commitments with the drive to run a business.

activity

The information about Aisling Collins, below, is on the Shell LiveWIRE website (www.shell-livewire.org). It is principally a promotional site for bean-there.com but, within the case study there are examples of Aisling showing the characteristics of an entrepreneur. Can you identify these characteristics?

Being successful

In your local community, there are successful businesses being run by people who have all or most of these characteristics. It is necessary to understand that in order for a business to be successful it does not have to be large and employ many people. A successful business is one which achieves its aims and makes money. For someone like Bill Gates of Microsoft, that aim was to have a PC on every desk and in every home and along the way that aim turned him into a multi-millionaire. A young person running a one-man flyer delivery service and making sufficient out of the business to support himself and his family is also successful. Certain characteristics are necessary for an entrepreneur but they alone do not make the business successful: it is also necessary to have a good idea!

CASE STUDY — Aisling Collins

Aisling Collins, winner of the Shell LiveWIRE Young Business Award 2002.

So, you're on holiday in the beautiful North-West of Ireland and you're three thousand miles from home – you need a good cup of coffee and an Internet terminal. Thanks to Aisling Collins, you can sit back, relax, send those electronic postcards, and discover all that there is to do in the region.

Aisling launched bean-there.com in July 2000. Located in the Diamond area of Derry city, this Internet café provides high speed Internet access for tourists, shoppers and local small businesses. The café has a modern design with seating capacity for 40 people. It boasts an extensive gourmet sandwich menu, including a wide range of speciality breads and wraps. Bean-there also supplies breakfast and lunch platters to local businesses.

Aisling noticed the increasing numbers of tourists in the city since the Good Friday Peace Agreement, and set about creating a business that meets the new visitors' needs. In order to add to her significant passing trade in the city's commercial centre, Aisling linked up with local tour guides and proposed the café as a stop along the city's historical walking tour route. Tourists can now have a break, contact home, gather information on the area, and even book visits to other attractions.

Future plans include the introduction of training courses, providing local people with information technology skills.

Source: www.shell-livewire.org

10. Building a business

This unit outlines the steps involved in building a business, from generating ideas to marketing the product or service.

Starting out

Most entrepreneurs start their business by copying, improving or changing an idea that already exists. They rarely create or invent a completely new product or service. It is easier to start with an idea that already exists – people are using the product or service, so you do not have the task of introducing something completely new and encouraging customers to try it. To start a business an entrepreneur has to first of all generate an idea, to become aware of a need that exists, or a new or novel way of providing a product or service.

Who will your product appeal to?

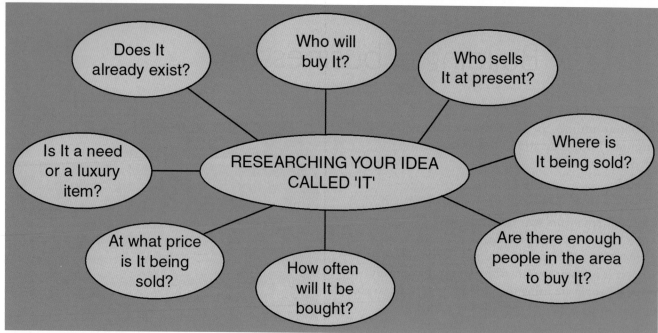

Think about it! Start with a mind map.

Researching your idea

You now have two ideas with which to work. At this point they are only ideas and you must carry out research in order to get a true picture of the need for your product or service.

Market sector

You have to decide on your **market sector**, to have an idea of who your customers could be. Some questions to consider are:

◆ Is your product appealing to one particular sex?

◆ Is it targeted at a particular age group (e.g., children, teenagers, young homemakers or elderly people)?

◆ Are there a sufficient number of people in this market sector living or working in the area in which you plan to locate your business? For example, if you are planning a window-cleaning service and identify working people and senior citizens as your market sector, you must provide your service in an area of high employment and one in which a high proportion of the residents are retired.

You must establish *who* is likely to be a potential customer. If you are going to be selling to a particular group of individuals you must find out their age, sex, marital status, occupation, income and lifestyle. You also need to know who within a couple makes or influences the buying decision. If your customer is a business you need to know its size, industry base, what products it buys, how often and what after-sales services it requires.

Knowing the four Ws

What people will buy:

◆ What kind? If you open an ice-cream parlour you must research your potential customers' taste for particular flavours, and work out what flavours are going to be most popular.

◆ What amount? If you were offering an ironing service you must find out approximately the number of items a customer will require ironing? If you were to run a car valet service you would need to know which level of service that you provide will be most used by your potential customers.

People will not always be aware of a need for a new product until the product is available. This is probably best explained by a famous quote from Henry Ford: 'If I had asked customers what they wanted they would have said a faster horse.'

When people will buy:

◆ Is your business seasonal? Will customers buy more at particular times of the year?

◆ How often can you expect repeat business?

◆ Would customers be attracted by incentives to encourage repeat business (e.g., loyalty cards)?

◆ Will there be a higher demand for your business at particular times of the week? For example, a taxi firm or a restaurant would expect to be busier on a weekend than on a Monday.

Where your customers prefer to buy:

◆ Do they like to buy from home, by phone, over the Internet or do they prefer to visit a shop?

◆ Do they want to buy at their place of work or do they want to buy where they live?

You decide on the location of your business by taking into account:

◆ Costs – being located on a high street will be much more expensive than further out of the town centre.

◆ Passing trade – how many people pass the location in an hour?

◆ Access – can delivery vans get in easily? Is there parking close by?

◆ Competition – how close is the nearest competitor? Is there a competitor on the same side of the street?

Why your customers will buy from you rather than your competitors:

◆ What will make your product or service more desirable than those that already exist?

If you are to succeed, your product and service must be much better than, or different to, that currently offered by your competitors. It may be that you intend to offer a superior service, more pleasant premises or keener prices, but it has to be different or better in order to persuade customers to come to you rather than to your competitors.

Businesses must provide what consumers want.

53

Use existing information

Use the Internet or your local library to access information and statistics that already exist. Invest Northern Ireland business information services (see unit 8, pages 44–5) and government-sponsored websites provide a wide range of easily understood information and statistics. Something as simple as the Yellow Pages provides information on businesses that exist in particular areas.

Competition

You must also research your competition, who you are going to have to compete with for customers. Visit or telephone their premises to establish exactly what they offer customers and how much they are charging. Take notice of good points you may not have thought of and pay particular attention to how you will be able to offer a better product or service. Also find out whether there is sufficient business available to support two businesses, as you do not want to be the one to lose out! Sometimes, however, being close to your competitor can be a good strategy, as people know to go to a particular area to find a particular product.

Scalini is one of the many restaurants and cafés on Belfast's Botanic Avenue.

activities

Work in the same group that came up with your two ideas in the activity on page 51.

1. Divide into two smaller groups, with each taking one of the ideas to research.
2. Research your idea.
3. Decide on your market sector.
4. Find out what similar businesses already exist in your area.
5. What are their strengths and weaknesses?
6. Plan how you are going to compete with them.
7. You may wish to draw up a questionnaire and carry out a survey of at least 20 people who you have identified as being part of your intended market sector. Remember to use the 'four Ws' in your research.
8. When you have completed your research, analyse your findings.
9. Working as a whole group again, decide which of the two ideas will be the better business proposition.

Questionnaires

The type of information you can find out from a questionnaire depends on how you ask the questions. You might need just numerical information, or you might require a deeper knowledge of the views of those questioned.

Quantitative research is a survey where everyone is asked the same set of questions and a numeric count is made of the answers. For example, if you were planning on opening an ice-cream parlour you could ask everyone: 'do you like strawberry ice cream?' If you have a sufficient positive response, you know you ought to stock strawberry ice cream.

Qualitative research allows people to discuss things. In a qualitative questionnaire the question could be: 'why do you like strawberry ice cream?' If your answers shows that people like to have pieces of strawberry fruit throughout the ice cream, you know you need to stock this type of ice cream or serve fresh strawberries in addition to the ice cream.

Designing your product or service

Having now decided on a particular product or service, you, as an entrepreneur, have to turn it into a business. You have identified your product or service; you have identified your market sector; now you have to give your idea an identity which makes it uniquely yours (i.e., something that makes it different to all others presently on the market).

Image

You must now decide what image you are going to give your product or service that will make it particularly appealing to the market sector you are going to target.

Is it going to fall into the useful, practical, and essential category or the luxurious, glamorous, and inspirational category? How you see your product or service determines how you design it. If it is in the useful category it ought to have a 'no frills' design, whereas if it is in the luxury category it ought to have a very expensive appearance.

activities

1. Make a full list of the characteristics of your product; for example, if your product is hairspray your list may contain such characteristics as: unperfumed, three different levels of holding strength, glitter version, different sized bottles, etc.

   If your business is going to be a service, make a full list of all the details of the service being provided. If, for example, you are planning a window-cleaning service, your list may contain such details as: doing ground-level windows only; doing two levels of windows; doing both inside and outside of windows; cleaning window frames as well as the glass; etc.

2. Clearly identify the characteristics that are unique to your item or service.

activity

Draw up a design brief for your product or service. This requires an outline drawing or prototype of the product with details of name, colour, cost, etc., or a defined list of your service with a name.

Packaging, design and name for tropical pure fruit juice with young children and health-conscious parents the target market.

SPECIFICATION

- Single size to contain 250 mls of juice.
- Family size to contain 1 litre of juice.
- Colour scheme to compliment tropical content and appeal to target market.
- Shape suitable for hand-size of young child.
- Container to be as spill-proof as possible.
- Emphasize the fruit content and contribution to dietary need.

Design brief for selling a tropical fruit drink.

55

Marketing your product or service

Marketing simply means how you are going to be selling your product or service. Marketing procedures are easily divided into four processes called the four Ps.

Product

◆ What product or service are you going to sell?

◆ What are the unique characteristics of your product or service?

You must identify these in order to be able to highlight these points in your promotion.

Place

This may be the premises from which you are going to sell your product or service, or perhaps the type of outlet you plan to sell from. For example, if shortbread was your product you may open your own shop specialising in different flavours of shortbread, or you may see large supermarket chains such as Tesco or Sainsbury's as being your customers.

You also need to decide what area you are going to sell your product or service to. For example, is it going to be restricted to one part of a particular town, a whole town or city, or will it be available all over Northern Ireland or internationally?

Finding the right price is essential.

Price

◆ How much do you intend to charge for your product or service? Remember, the price must cover costs as well as allow some profit.

◆ How much are your competitors charging? Remember, if an item appears to be too cheap, customers may be put off buying as they may consider it to be inferior.

◆ Do you plan any introductory offers? If so, what is your long-term pricing plan?

SINGLE USE GOODS	DURABLE GOODS	SERVICES
These are throwaway goods that are consumed with use. These goods are bought often.	Goods that have a long lifespan and are generally bought when they need replacing.	Buying the service and expertise of others. These may be frequently used or used only once or occasionally.

Types of products or services.

Brand names and logos help to promote products.

Promotion

Where and how are you going to promote your product or service? If you are restricted to a particular area, your advertising ought to be restricted to the same area. Likewise, if your product or service has a local flavour and is aimed specifically at a Northern Irish market there is no point in advertising nationally.

You may feel that you ought to have a logo to identify your business.

You must also take your market sector into account when deciding on your promotional themes and providers. For example, it is no use using senior citizens in an advertisement for a product that is aimed at the teenage market.

activity

You have been awarded a grant of £5,000 from the Prince's Trust NI to start your business. You must decide how much of this you are going to allocate to marketing, and draw up a plan of how this allocation is to be spent.

Being enterprising

Throughout this unit we have tried to engage in the activities of being enterprising. We have tried to turn an idea into a business. All over the country people have ideas for starting a business. It has been said that if all ideas were turned into businesses we would be a nation of entrepreneurs, rather than a nation that relies heavily on the public sector for employment.

It is unfortunate that when an idea is born it can be killed off almost immediately by a smirk, scorn, lack of interest or enthusiasm from the first person it is suggested to. Those who have ideas are the creative people who bring about new developments for us all. These people are the geniuses of business as they are the creative ones, but they also need the help and support available from the different agencies that exist to give support to new businesses (see pages 44–45).

There is now a wealth of support available in Northern Ireland to those who have a good idea and wish to start a new business. All of us who have an idea ought to take the opportunity provided by these agencies to see if our idea could work. Taking the first step is the hardest. We do not want to feel foolish, but if we do not try we will never know if what is an idea today could be a successful business in the future.

11. Skills and qualities

This unit outlines how your own skills and qualities could enable you to be enterprising.

Running a business of your own requires certain skills and qualities. While many of us have these, we may not yet possess them at the level required to be successful as an entrepreneur. When you recognise that you possess some or all of these qualities and skills you can develop them over a period of time.

What skills and qualities do you have that would enable you to be enterprising?

Independence, motivation and determination

- Do you have an independent spirit?
- Are you motivated and determined?
- Do you manage to complete tasks set for you in school on your own or do you have to rely on friends or others in your group to motivate, encourage and support you?
- When you are given a project to complete do you see it as a challenge and look forward to finding the necessary information and presenting it in an interesting way?
- Do you hope to come up with a new approach or slant to the task set?
- Can you accept that not all people are prepared to treat you as a young adult when you seek information and still continue to explore until you get what you want?

Running your own business can be lonely, so you need to be self-motivated, self-reliant and determined to succeed. You need to be prepared for upsets and refusals but still be determined to continue.

Could you keep going when success seems to elude you? Sahar Hashemi, listed as one of the top 100 business women in the UK, founded the Coffee Republic chain of specialist coffee shops and introduced the coffee trend in the United States to

You need to be determined to succeed.

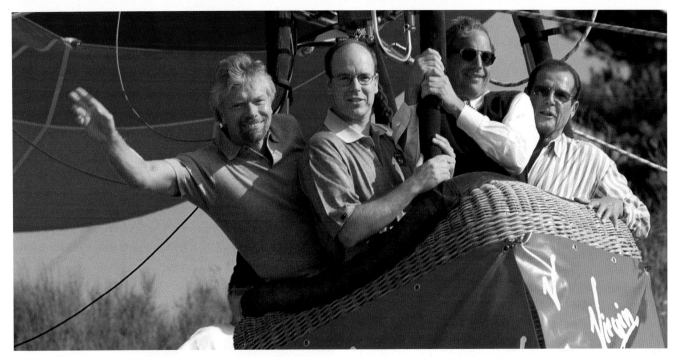

Entrepreneur Richard Branson attempting to go round the world in a hot-air balloon. He keeps failing but he keeps trying!

Great Britain. She has warned that you almost have to fail by 99 per cent before you get there.

Would you have the determination to continue if you appeared to be failing? To fail 99 per cent means only a 1 per cent success rate. When you work hard in preparing for a test in school and don't perform as well as you had hoped, are you still determined to do better in the next test? Do you talk to your teacher to see how you could improve your work and your revision methods? Do you keep going until you reach your target? When playing sport if your team is being beaten badly do you give up trying or do you increase your determination to stop that ball crossing your defence line again? In running a business it is necessary to have determination to succeed, and not to give up but to build on that 1 per cent success rate.

Patience and resilience

It takes time for a business to build a **customer base** and for people to accept change and move to something new. The person pushing this change as his or her business idea needs, therefore, to be patient, to allow customers time to come round to the new idea. Resilience is required to keep going, to accept very limited or no success and still continue to persist with the idea. You need to be able to keep playing the game to the best of your ability even when you are making little or no progress. Continued effort will bring success.

Realism

A person must also be realistic in the goals he or she sets. Being realistic is knowing your strengths and weaknesses. Then you must learn to use your strengths to the full and avoid areas where you are weak, but, at the same time, try to overcome your weaknesses. It takes time to develop a business. Success will not be achieved overnight. Being realistic is not expecting to be an instant millionaire, but expecting to gain only a small, if any, profit in the early years of the business. Being realistic is expecting to have to commit many hours of work over and above the norm to achieve success.

activity

Design a poster (A4 size) encouraging young people who have the qualities of determination, motivation and a spirit of independence to become entrepreneurs. If you have access to a computer it would be useful for this activity.

Confidence and self-belief

◆ Are you confident?

◆ Can you present yourself to others in a manner which impresses them and makes them consider you to be a confident young adult?

◆ Do you have belief in yourself and your abilities?

As an entrepreneur you will have to have sufficient faith in yourself and your idea to convince others that your business idea will be successful. Could you convince a bank manager that your idea will work, that you have carried out the necessary research to succeed and that you have planned the progress of your business properly so that he/she believes that they ought to provide finance for your new business? You have to be completely focused on your idea and your belief which, supported by research and planning, has to give you the confidence to get the necessary financial support. Have you the determination to try, try, and try again when faced with refusal after refusal from banks and financial institutions?

Remember, if what you are planning to do is such a wonderful idea, and will be so successful, why has it not been done before? Why are hundreds of people not being highly successful at doing the same thing? It takes a great deal of confidence to face many refusals and still continue to be positive. It is this determined belief in your idea and the confidence to pursue it that will bring about success. Sahar Hashemi (see page 58) had 22 refusals when she sought finance to open her first coffee shop, but she believed in her idea, had confidence that it would succeed, persisted and became highly successful.

activity

Being confident is a strength, but if you become over-confident you run the risk of being arrogant. Arrogance would not be helpful to an entrepreneur. Working as a group, discuss why you think this is so.

Entrepreneurs need to be flexible.

Flexibility

It is also necessary for an entrepreneur to have flexibility: to learn from mistakes and be prepared to change if things can be done in a better way to what was originally planned. Flexibility is being able to listen to and respond to suggestions and ideas from others and being able to move in a different direction when an opportunity occurs. For example, when a class is having difficulty understanding a particular point you will see the teacher use a different approach in order to help the class understand.

Humility

- Do you always admit to not understanding a particular point in a lesson?
- Do you ask your teacher to explain it again?
- Do you ask a family member or a friend to help you with something you are unsure of?

Humility is necessary; you must not be afraid to seek help and advice, afraid to admit to being unsure of how to do something, or afraid of appearing to be a failure. For an entrepreneur, listening to and accepting advice is a quality that is essential in order to avoid costly mistakes. Accepting that others have more experience and knowledge than you and seeking their help and support is essential.

Responsible and reliable

- Are you responsible and reliable?
- Do you keep the promises you make?
- Do you complete work by the set date?
- Do you turn up for training or practice as instructed?

We may do these things when prompted, encouraged, bribed or threatened by family or friends but being responsible and reliable are qualities that we all ought to strive to develop fully. As an entrepreneur you must be responsible and reliable. You will be your own boss. You will have to make your own decisions and work to your own timetable. There will be no one there to check on you. It is up to you to be responsible and do the necessary work. Customers must know you are reliable: they must know that your business will be open at the stated times, that you will do a good job and complete the work on time.

Stamina and sacrifices

- When the going gets tough do you quit or do you keep going?
- Do you always keep going until you have completed a task?

As an entrepreneur you have to have stamina to make that extra effort to continue. This may well mean extra hours of work in a week which will require sacrifices from you. If you have to work late you may not be able to socialise with your friends or family in the same way. You may not be able to leave your business to go on holiday. You may have to commit part of your weekends to completing paperwork and making preparations for the following week. The difficult part of this may be convincing family and friends that they are not being neglected, but that, at that particular time, the business has to have priority.

activity

We have now looked at the key qualities and skills of an entrepreneur. Make a list of these and give occasions when you showed you had these qualities. These may be occasions when you were in class at school or taking part in school events. They could also be occasions when you were working part-time or when you were at a social gathering.

Using your skills and qualities

Each of us has some of these skills and qualities to a greater or lesser extent. Some of us may be fortunate enough to have all of them; others may have some of them, while the remainder of us have a few of them.

While these are qualities and skills necessary to an entrepreneur, perhaps because they make him or her a person who is respected and trusted, they are also qualities and skills that if properly developed will enhance the lives of all of us.

No matter what route we take in life – to be an entrepreneur, an employee, an entrepreneurial employer or employee – to be respected and trusted in what we do in life is something each of us should strive towards.

activity

Discuss each of the points of the Schools Soccer League plan (below) and identify the entrepreneurial qualities and skills involved in each point.

CASE STUDY

Schools Soccer League

We can do better!

Ballysmalltown High School has been bottom of the Schools Soccer League for the last five years. A new coach has just been appointed. He has drawn up a five-year development plan for the team which includes the following points:

◆ Training will be held each Monday and Wednesday afternoon from 3.00–4.30 pm, including some school holidays. Attendance at training is essential. Non-attendance without a legitimate excuse will result in the player not taking part in the next game.

◆ Kits in a new design and colours will be purchased with the help of the PTA.

◆ The aim for the end of the first season is to move at least four places up the league table.

◆ Each match is to be treated as an individual event.

◆ Members of the squad will take part in a fitness regime as part of training. Each person will be encouraged to improve his personal level of fitness and to keep a record of his success.

◆ Team meetings and debriefings will be held before and after each match when each player will have an opportunity to contribute.

◆ This development plan will be reviewed at the end of each season.

◆ Opportunities will be taken to send squad members on specialist coaching courses.

Glossary

Accredited to be officially recognised as having achieved specific standards or qualities.

Action what needs to be done to achieve the outcomes of the targets.

Automated assembly lines where goods are made in stages by computer-operated machinery.

Capital cost the cost of buying items such as machinery or equipment which will be used for many years within a business.

Catalyst the thing, person or event that brings about a change.

Creative thinking the ability to come up with a different/new way of approaching a task.

Customer base the group of regular customers who form the foundation of a business.

Curriculum vitae a personally designed document which sets out the main details about yourself.

Employability the possession by an individual of the qualities and competences required to meet the changing needs of employers and customers and thereby helping to realise his or her aspirations and potential to work.

Entrepreneur one who undertakes a business opportunity with the intention of making profit.

Genetically modified crops deliberate modification of crops by the use of genes from another species in order to obtain such things as improved insect-resistance, 'vaccination' against specific diseases or longer 'shelf life'.

Global economy the organisation and distribution of production in countries throughout the world.

Goal-setting this is when you decide on outcomes which you will then work towards.

Imagery use of pictures, personalities and style of presentation in order to portray a particular idea or image.

Income tax a tax which is paid by individuals on all income over a specified amount.

Innovation the development an idea which has not been developed before.

Interpersonal skills people skills that include persuasion and influence, negotiation, communication, giving feedback, sensitivity and delegation.

Lifelong learning continuous learning throughout your life, the development of existing skills, along with new qualifications.

Margins the extra amounts which are added to the costs of an item in order to arrive at the selling price.

Market sector the section or group of consumers within a particular market to whom your product will appeal.

Mass production the production of goods in large quantities.

Modern apprenticeships a pathway in employment and training for 16-21 year olds.

Niche market a section or group of people who fall into a particular category due to interests, characteristics or a set of conditions.

Opportunity cost the cost of having to do without one item because you chose to buy another.

Organic goods that are produced without the use of any artificial fertilisers or pesticides.

Public sector the section of the economy which is run by government in order to provide public services such as education and health.

Raw materials materials such as cotton, cereals, or wood which are used in the production of goods.

Retail selling of goods to the consumer for personal use.

Review examination of situation at present time in order to decide how to move forward.

Social costs the costs incurred by businesses in order to ensure that their methods and practices are acceptable to the society in which they operate.

Socially responsible to willingly comply to a way of life which has regard for other people, their property and the environment in which they live.

Target-setting this is the process of breaking the goal up into manageable steps so that each step becomes SMART targets.

Transferable skills skills that are developed within one situation and then applied to other situations.

Index